THE BURQA AND THE MINISKIRT

The suicide terrorists Fertility power and progress

ANGELO BERTOLO

authorHOUSE®

AuthorHouse™ UK
1663 Liberty Drive
Bloomington, IN 47403 USA
www.authorhouse.co.uk
Phone: 0800.197.4150

Published by AuthorHouse 04/01/2016

ISBN: 978-1-5246-3086-7 (sc)
ISBN: 978-1-5246-3087-4 (hc)
ISBN: 978-1-5246-3085-0 (e)

FOREWORD

Unusual perspectives are always more interesting than hackneyed and clichéd ones. Ever since the days of Malthus, population growth and fertility increases have been regarded as big problems, especially for developing countries. There has been there odd economist like Julian Simon who has questioned this basic proposition. However, that remains the exception rather than the norm. Population increases at a geometric rate, but food production only increases at an arithmetic rate. Malthus' ghost does not die easily, even though Malthus himself revised his rigid position somewhat in subsequent editions of his "Essay".

There ought to be a difference between rabbits and humans. The correlation between demographic transition and economic growth is at best complex. Medical advances, better food distribution and the end of war reduce death rates. That much is obvious. However, birth rates take longer to drop. That much is also obvious. India is a case in point. The 1981 Census showed a drop in birth rates in Kerala and there was continuing debate about what this decline was due to and how this could be replicated in other Indian States. The 1991 Census showed a similar decline in Tamil Nadu and by no stretch of the imagination was this a replication of the Kerala model. The 2001 Census extended the success to Andhra Pradesh and 2011 is bound to show similar declines in Karnataka. Birth rates are more a function of awareness, female literacy and availability of potable water than of per capita income or family planning programmes and contraceptive methods. In that sense, there is a difference between a contraceptive policy and a population policy.

Any economics textbook on developmental economics will describe population growth as a major problem for developing economies like India. Ask any economist, what determines output growth and the answer will be land, labour, capital and entrepreneurship. If labour is an input and its marginal product is not zero, presumably labour is not necessarily a bad thing. Why is population then a problem? In addition, entrepreneurship does not function without labour. Nor do technological improvements or productivity increases, estimated as a residual after netting out labour and capital growth estimates in econometric studies. The Malthusian prescription of population being a problem is based on two premises. First, there will be a shortage of land or other exhaustible resources. This proposition has doubtful empirical validity. It fails to anticipate productivity increase, human ingenuity, technological advances and discovery of new resources. Second, much of the population is useless in the sense of producing a zero (perhaps even negative) marginal product. Hence, if one could eliminate some of the population, the denominator in per capita income would decline and with a constant numerator, per capita income would increase. A country with a smaller population would be richer. This proposition has even more doubtful empirical validity. True, the productivity of the population is a function of access to education and wealth. It is also true that most developing countries have serious governance problems of providing education and health services, which is why the Millennium Development Goals (set for 2015) seem even more distant. Other than education and health, there are also governance problems associated with urban planning and providing physical infrastructure like power, transportation and roads. However, both for physical and social infrastructure, the problem remains one of governance, not of population growth. Population is a bogey.

As was mentioned, population growth in India is slowing down. The present rate is 1.9% per year and is due to slow down to 1.5% in the next ten years, with significant inter-regional variations. This means that the dependency ratio is declining, also because babies born twenty or twenty five years ago are now entering the labour force. If India now aspires to a 8% GDP (gross domestic product) growth rate in the next ten years, anything between 1% and 2% of per capita income growth will be due to this labour component. Somewhat more arguably, in the former Soviet Union, productivity levels have always been low. The perestroika problem of diminishing returns to capital wouldn't have become so significant had it not been for the simultaneous phenomenon of labour input declines.

Professor Angelo Bertolo is not an economist. He is a historian and his perspective in this monograph is that of a historian, with a very broad canvas. Stated simply, the proposition advanced is the following. *Humanity progresses when the birth rate is high. Humanity regresses when the birth rate is low.* There is a product life cycle in evolution of civilizations and Professor Bertolo finds a direct correlation between decline and fall and demographic transition. The canvas covered includes Greece, Rome, Great Britain, ancient India and Sumeria, and makes for a compelling argument. There is a yet another argument which economists might refer to as the positive externality argument associated with a large population. Here Professor Bertolo's rhetorical question. "Would India be a great country, a world power, if the population were only one hundred and fifty million with a GNP comparable to Britain's?" The question is rhetorical and indeed, the answer is no. India would not even be India, or China what is China today. Externalities associated with political power transcend economic indicators alone.

This may seem to be a novel idea, as indeed it is. But it is precisely because all interesting ideas are novel that this monograph should be read. There is much to think about it.

Bibek Debroy
Director
Rajiv Gandhi Institute For Contemporary Studies
Rajiv Gandhi Foundation
New Delhi, February 2003

Bibek Debroy is an Indian economist but his cultural background is strong. He is not the simple accountant that knows the figures of the economy of a country. He knows both the comprehensive history of India and of the West. He translated from Sanscrit into English most of the ancient epic poems, and wrote interesting essays on poetry philosophy and religion. With this background, which can be compared to our comprehensive humanistic background, he was able to understand the relationship between birth rates and progress, and the fact that the economy is only one aspect of the history of man in this earth, though an important one.

MURDERCIDE

Scientific American, January 2006: *Murdercide, Science unravels the myth of suicide murders*, by Michael Shermer

All the information about the suicide bombers in this article seems to me pertinent and appropriate. Congratulations for the accurate psychology, and the status, of the suicide bombers. I find the fact that suicide bombers are generally not poor, uneducated, disaffected or disturbed as commonly thought particularly appropriate. They usually come from upper or middle classes, from caring intact families, many are married with children and are professionals or semiprofessionals. Quite surprisingly very few have any background in religion, or in the humanities. It is also interesting to notice that many come from countries like Saudi Arabia and Bahrain which are economically well off yet lacking in civil liberties.

However, there is one aspect that the author of the column Michael Shermer seems not to be able to grasp in full, and maybe also political scientist Ami Pedahzur of the University of Haifa who is quoted in the article: the historical context of a developing civilization, of populations that are not yet fully mature but that are bound to be so in the future, a moment in their growth, in their evolution, when **"men feel with perturbated soul, with perturbated emotions"**, when sentiments are high and often irrational, before the time when they will be able to "reflect with pure reason" - according to the philosophical concepts of history first expressed by G.B. Vico (1668-1744) and later by German and French philosophers of history. This time of aggressive **perturbated and irrational sentiments** is a phase of great progress for them, a great leap forward in many human activities (although much less so in creating science) -- **together with another datum** that Scientific American columnists, the media and also many universities not only in the west are unwilling to acknowledge because ideology blinds people in spite of evidence --- **together with a high birth rate** of the same population. Not only the ideology of Islam blinds people, also the secular ideology of family planning programs blinds people's minds, in spite of statistical and historical evidence.

Other peoples, other civilizations showed similar irrational behaviour when they were in a similar phase of growth, of evolution, although they showed it in different ways, with a different "personality", as every civilization shows a different personality in the arts. The Muslim peoples are showing this "progress" in this historical moment in their peculiar way also with the suicide bombers – they count in the world today more than one or two generations ago, while the more rational west with lower birth rates counts always less. The Japanese showed a somewhat similar aggressive attitude in the first part of the 20th century. The Puritans in England and in America were similarly irrational and aggressive in the 17th century, a time of great progress for them, and also of high birth rates. The time of aggressive and perturbated emotions is a time of irrationality and also of genius, of poetry, a time when "men create religions", or reinforce their irrational moral sense. Not yet a time of rationality, and of science.

It is their irrational moral sense, these young men and women that sacrifice their lives with a bomb in view of an irrational ideal that we westerners cannot understand, these girls that go to school in Europe wearing their irrational clothes, not miniskirts, -- that in the end will be the winners over a decadent, and dying, European civilization.

May I make a comparison and draw a parallel in anthropological terms with a phenomenon which I notice in the Catholic church both in the west and in developing countries: some young men and women from positive intact caring and often numerous families are endowed with high ideals towards God, and are ready to sacrifice their lives not with a bomb but with the almost irrational vows of chastity poverty and obedience, and dedicate their lives to God and to their neighbour. In case of martyrdom but even without, they are proclaimed saints as an example to future generations - while murderciders in muslim countries appear in posters like star athletes to be imitated.

THE "ARAB SPRINGS"

In January 2011 I was in Indonesia, and news arrived about uprisings: in Tunisia, then in Egypt, then in Libya, and even in Syria. They were uprisings against their governments, not against westerners, and not even of a purely religious nature. But deep down they also reflect Islamic fundamentalism. My Chinese friend, Doctor Lie, who is president of the industrialists in Medan, Sumatra, tells me that he is worried something like this could happen in Indonesia as well; people could rebel against corrupt governments, who don't act in the interest of the people.

When I returned to Italy I heard about this "Arab Spring" in more detail, and I would like to offer a comment of my own, purely personal, one you don't hear on the media in Italy or America.

I observe that the people are rebelling against their governing bodies, against the corruption of those in power. A rebellion that can be considered of social value, since they stand against the privileged classes that are most prominent today, against a particular dictator, against the powerful. In the West we would say that it is a revolution in the democratic sense, for more democracy, for better social justice. But this is only the beginning, an initial motivation. Extreme Islam is always present, as a common motivation that stimulates everything .

I observe that these demonstrations also have a religious aspect, even though this doesn't seem the main motive. Those who demonstrate or fight against the current tyrant are motivated by a nationalistic spirit that also has a religious side. The moral and religious sense strengthens with irrational demonstrations of intolerance against what is different. In some countries the rebels seem to have already reached their goal to overthrow the tyrant. In Syria, instead, the tyrant resists. In all Muslim countries of the Middle East there was a notable number of Christians a few years ago, with minorities that contributed to the general social well-being – well-being as we westerners see it. Now Christians are the outsiders, they're persecuted and they have to flee. This is not a new phenomenon – it has happened throughout history, and also not in Muslim areas. But it began with these particular characteristics a few years ago, and now it has become more dramatic . In Syria the Christians minority cannot agree completely with the governing class. However, under the current regime Christians are tolerated, they are an integral part of the country. If the regime falls and the rebels take over, Christians will certainly be persecuted more than before.

In the 1970s I gathered information about Iran and the Shah from people who had lived and worked there, but I didn't pay sufficient attention to the phenomenon of the Ayatollah Khomeini, to the new religious awakening of the Iranians, in the nationalistic sense. Some of the people who had left Iran thought Khomeini was a criminal, evil. Which could be true, and could be said for Colonel Gadaffi, too. But the rebellion against Gadaffi and Mubarak today can be considered similar and parallel to the movement against the Shah in the 70s and 80s. Today Iran is one of the few countries in the world that encourages demographic growth, to augment the population. They want to double the current population to 81 million, for imperialistic reasons. It's a sign of faith in their future. Like Fascism in Italy.

There are laws of natural physics (Newton's apple falling to the ground), and there are also laws in the evolution of human nature, of civilization, in populations that grow and evolve in the course of history. Laws of psychological character, and not only that. One of these laws is that populations, civilizations, grow, gain political pre-eminence, dominate, and then fall. They don't remain forever in a position of political and cultural pre-eminence. One of the phenomena tightly linked to growth (material progress and increased political and military importance) is high fertility, population increase. And Muslim populations in this particular historical moment, are fertile. Another factor, closely related to this, is the reinforcement of a moral and religious sense. Often, as in this case, with irrational manifestations of an aggressive nature. At times, however, without aggression a moral strengthening in a broader sense. Islam as a religion, in this case, would give a social bonding among all populations, as if it were the other face of the aggressive nationalism that had been active in Europe recently.

These are not aspects peculiar to Islam, they have been apparent in many other human areas before now. In Europe a century ago, even in a culturally Christian environment. It's the concept for which mankind creates religions. And if these religions aren't created at all, these ideologies, which are artificial religions, give a push to existing religions and moral sense. (This is a delicate concept, one expressed by G. B. Vico and by German philosophers from Feuerbach after him. A concept that I just want to mention briefly.)

One of the first things we can observe: 1) A high demographic increase in those populations, which is a symptom of progress, seen in a broader sense of evolution and growth; 2) The strengthening of a moral and religious sense that seems irrational to us in the West, a strengthening that appears diametrically opposed to the weakening of a moral sense in our Western culture, which is a sign of decadence and regression for the West; 3) The minority appears to be the most extreme, while many, perhaps the majority, tend to be more moderate. But this minority is the one that leads the masses, that influences the masses. They're the ones who distinguish themselves, destined to prevail, the base of a new g dominating social class; 4) A distinguishing feature of Islam: religion and political life are one, a spirit that animates populations, like patriotism, love of fatherland and a sense of racial superiority stimulated us a century ago, the imperialism that brought on two world wars. A dominant ideology, that of the fatherland, that can be considered an artificial religion. Ideology – religion created by man – religion that is destined to evolve and become preeminent, but not to exist forever.

In Europe, in our culture, we've had similar phenomena before. The Protestant Reform in northern Europe. We note an irrational (heretic) reinforcement of the moral and religious sense. An irrational energetic shift of the moral sense against the corruption of the Roman church. John Calvin burnt more witches than all the popes of his time. Martin Luther is a moral figure in a nationalistic sense. We can observe the political, military and economical rising and consolidation of those societies : all the countries of Northern Europe in the 16th century. We also observe *en passant* the affirmation of local languages. Calvin in the 16th Century, Khomeini in 1980 can be easily compared.

Earlier, after the year 1000, there was a similar, irrational and violent reinforcement of the moral and religious sense in the South of Europe, a similar violent moral shift against the corruption of Rome. Heresies arose. It was the time when the spirit of man was "moved and troubled" ("*avvertiscono con animo perturbato e commosso*"), often in a violent way, but not always . . . Francis of Assisi was certainly not rational, but equally certainly, not violent. But "his spirit was_moved and troubled", as Vico would say. Catari and Albigesi were also violent, and troubled and_moved. It all ended with a genocide, not with their political affirmation, as it might have, had men and luck performed differently. Even Martin Luther and the Anglo-Saxon reformers of the 16th and 17th centuries were in that same condition – troubled and moved – and were often violent. Two historical periods, just after 1000 in the South, and after the 16th century in the North, during which these countries evolved and began to grow, politically and culturally . Periods with irrational manifestations, with violence, with the development of languages, of poetry. A couple of centuries later, in the South, these populations became more rational. For southern Europe, Italy in particular, the Renaissance was to be the period during which "men reflect with a pure mind" – according to the concept of Vico. And in the same way contemporary, modern society, faced with developing populations, is more rational. (*En passant*, the development of language and poetry, the *langue d'oc*, *Cantico delle creature* by Francis of Assisi, poetry and religious sense in Dante. And with the Protestant Reform, affirmation of the language of Luther, and the Elizabethans.)

It's the same type of phenomenon that is happening today in developing countries. Countries that are predestined to prevail, over us as well. But if luck changes, very grave events could occur in the near future. Events that can be compared to the two world wars, to the Crusades of Albigeses, to genocide. Otherwise, they might impose themselves and be successful. Like the Protestants in Northern Europe. But there are other developing populations, in Asia, which seem to have some initial advantage over populations of Muslim religion. China and India, with different religions, and with civil ideals that can be compared to artificial religions imposed by governments. Political bonders, ideologies similar to religions. In the Islamic world the great majority seems to express violent and irrational attitudes. But there are also sincerely religious and non-violent figures. Roughly speaking, a pattern, an almost geometric model, is reproduced, one which was revealed with the violent reinforcement of the moral and religious sense with medieval heresies first, then later with the heresy of the Protestant Reform. With this way of interpreting history (it's not important for us which sense of heresy), the sense of the correct interpretation of the Scriptures, the general sense of a moral standard. Men who are "moved and troubled" are the ones who create the moral standard. And they impose it through violence.

And if one of these hotheads were to use the atomic bomb? Against Israel, or others? Even as a single suicidal act.

No comment.

I read with interest, and worry, magazines such as the American *Foreign Affairs*, or the Italian *Limes*. At this level, no one seems to have any comment to make about the facts of history and human life. With the parameters of an historical philosopher. I read about American political experts, Hillary Clinton in particular, former Secretary of State, at present presidential candidate. Mrs Clinton is well-informed about the Middle East, she knows how well-armed terrorists are, how strong they are, who collaborates with America and who is two-faced. She is informed about everything but she doesn't understand what's going on. She wants to export democracy to the Arab countries. She wants to export the values and the mentality of a West that is in decline, and that other countries hate and despise. A West that has lost almost all its vital driving force. She wants to hold on to American interests in the area. A similar President of the United States would accelerate the complete fall of the nation – without understanding what's going on. Not even in America.

I have no political advice to give. However, I would invite anyone who has a certain amount of influence on political life and history, of single countries, too – our countries as well – to reflect on what happened in Europe (we could limit our attention to England) in the 16th and 17th centuries. New ideas, of a religious and moral character, arrived In England from Northern Europe, which suggested possible political advantages to Henry

VIII: freedom from the cultural predominance of Rome, reinforcement of his institutional position, the possibility of taking over the wealth of the Church. Without really understanding what was happening, his daughter Mary persecuted and fought Protestants, without much success. Her sister Elizabeth, shrewd and astute, was better able to interpret the sentiments of the majority . She avoided gratuitous provocation and aimed for the good of England. Oliver Cromwell comes over as a religious Puritan, while Charles I was unaware of what was happening. But Cromwell had his logic. He imposed his dictatorial regime, but aimed mainly at the social and political interests of his country. The Puritans were hotheads, extremists, but they, too, evolved, both in England and in America, with intelligent personalities like Oliver Cromwell, and the Founding Fathers of America. And they were at the heart of all the development, the progress in England and America in the following centuries. We observe again, *en passant,* the fanatic and irrational moral and religious sense of the Puritans and the Calvinists which was a fundamental factor in their economic and political progress and success. And we also observe the high birthrate at the heart of their success, as well as the political intelligence of several figures who were able to work over and above the religious and moral concepts which were at the base of their push, of their vital force, towards a near future. We also can observe that the new attitudes and ideas of the Reform were not an absolute good; they were the manifestation of evolution, of internal changes of all mankind, not just the political or social area. We note that outstanding men, remaining firmly English in character, still were faithful to the Roman Catholic Church: Thomas More and William Shakespeare, for example.

I would suggest to a politician of today, one from our Western society, or one from a developing country: Look at what the starting situation was some time ago, observe the fundamental ideals as they were and as they are where you are functioning today. Look at what happened in England and in Northern Europe in the two historical periods we have been examining in a cursory way. Imagine yourself in the position of one of the contenders on either side (as Machiavelli did). Make parallels with the situation you're facing today. And act while you look ahead and behind. Don't believe that your ideals and your cultural position are absolutely superior to your adversary... but don't believe the opposite, either. Look back at the situation in the 12th and 13th centuries, rampant with hotheads, ready to kill and be killed, for their ideas. Ready to plot, as they do today. Don't believe the situation to be entirely different. Not even genocide. Not even collective suicide in the name of an ideal, of a religion. There are certainly differences. You will have to make your evaluation by means of your intelligence, your intuition.

(Final note. The real truth in a religious sense? Let's set it aside for the moment, while we discuss politics, history, human affairs, earthly interests. The real truth has its own value; the God who is part of history, who is in our midst. We are at a different level of comprehension. The Pope is right to attempt a dialogue with other religions. It's that quality that we characterize as "that extra something". It's difficult to compare it to other factors that are purely political or developmental.

If a wealthy Sheik with political clout, or if a friendly or unfriendly foreign state, organized a radio or television station like CNN or Al Jazeera, and broadcast information and news about the Koran with a scientific, western-style exegesis, as we do for the Bible – what might happen? The reaction would be furious. There would be murder. And what are they doing now? In the long haul, this could eventually bring about an Islamic Enlightenment, a laceration within Islam, with unimaginable consequences. Which seems already to be.)

CHENNAI CONFERENCE: BIRTH RATES AND PROGRESS

In the course of the five thousand years of history we know, from the Sumerians, to the Babylonians, to the Greeks, to the Romans, to our contemporary world; in the long eras which belong to the pre-historic period, in civilizations which are not part of our Western world, we can identify interesting patterns in the evolution of the various civilizations. There are epochs characterized by a high birth rate, high fertility and an increase in the population, and other epochs during which there is low fertility and a decrease in the population due to intrinsic causes and also to external factors such as epidemics or wars. Throughout history there is evident scientific and technological progress and a close examination will show that scientific, technological and economic progress, together with environmental conquests, also in a political sense, of dominance over other populations, always occur in strict relationship with a high birth-rate. In contrast, a low birth rate always precedes the decline and the end of a civilization, of a population, of an organized group of individuals. This decline implies the loss of scientific and technical knowledge and a degeneration in the economic standard of living, the loss of territories, not only politically, to more vigorous and successful populations, but also in the geographical and physical sense that the engineers of that population lose the mastership of their environment.

Together with this concept as if it were a law of nature, a law of physics, there are other factors that are closely related to it: the reinforcement of the moral and religious sense with irrational manifestations, or the diminishing of the moral standards before decadence; and the formation or dissolution of social classes. Irrationality in one phase, and rationality, pure reason, are both integral part human nature.

Let us consider the whole of humanity as though it were one civilization only:

1798, the catastrophic predictions of Malthus.

1830, the human population reached its first milliard of individuals.

1930, second milliard.

1961, third milliard.

1975, fourth milliard.

1987, fifth milliard.

1999, sixth milliard.

2011 welcome seven billion.

In this period was there evidence of scientific and technological progress all over the world, in parallel with demographic growth? Certainly. Like a law of nature. Like Newton's law in physics, in which he states that the apple does not fall to the ground but it is attracted by the ground, while the apple, in its turn, attracts the ground. Have the theories of Thomas Malthus proved to be completely mistaken? There is more food available for every single person in the world today than there was in Thomas Malthus' time. There is more food available for every child in India than there was in 1947, the year of her independence, with a population today three times as large. Even so it would not be right for us to say that Malthus was completely wrong. He represents the fears and the problems which man has always had.

From 1947, the year of her Independence, to 2000, the population in India increased threefold; that in Pakistan fourfold. The population in China, too, and in other Asiatic countries, has grown notably. On the contrary, from the Second World War to today the population in Europe has not shown a large increase in numbers. This is due more to secondary factors such as better medical services and an improved economy, than to intrinsic factors, to a high fertility. In proportion, India and the Asiatic countries have progressed more compared to Europe. They count more in the world politically than they did at the end of the Second World War.

External factors can contribute towards the numerical increase of a population, factors which are important but they are secondary, induced phenomena. Improved methods of agriculture help to nourish more people on the same territory; improved medical care helps them to survive. The medical world today, urged on by modern ideologies, actually helps towards diminishing the population, not only in China with her one-child policy.

As important as they may be, these are induced phenomena and their importance is secondary.

My region, Friuli, has a population today of around one million inhabitants. In Roman times, the moment of its maximum expansion, Aquileia had at least two hundred thousand inhabitants, perhaps only one hundred thousand. The population of Concordia reached at least thirty thousand. In the whole region we can find traces of the Roman methods of dividing up the land and remains of numerous villas. The region possessed a discreet population, possibly less than the actual million, but the standard of living was good, with local industries and a productive agriculture. The bridges, the roads and the buildings were of good quality. Caesar's legions who were fighting the Gauls came to Aquileia to pass the winter. The movement of the troops was quick and efficient, as in the times of Napoleon, the roads were surfaced, and they used horses and carts. Then the population began to diminish - this even before the arrival of the barbarians. The Romans were no longer able to master nature, its rivers and its marshes, and then the barbarians contributed in destroying the populations and the territory. By the heart of the Middle Ages, towards the year 1000, the population had decreased considerably - almost to the point of vanishing altogether. The economic life of the region was at its extremes. When did life in northern Italy begin to flourish again? In the centuries following the year 1000, with a return to life, with an increase in the population (information obtained from simple scholastic text books compiled for Italian high schools in the 1950's, Saitta e Giuliano Procacci among others). When was the technology of the Roman ships surpassed in the new historical epoch? With the steam engine in England in the 18th century, during the Industrial Revolution, a period of great technological progress, characterized also by a substantial demographic increase.

Progress, however, is not synonymous with **Happiness.**

National Geographic published another interesting article on the Indus Valley Civilisation (June 2000). There is not as much evidence regarding the Harappa civilisation as there is for the civilisations of Egypt and Mesopotamia, as we have not yet been able to decipher their writing. Yet scholars and archaeologists are puzzled at the fact of the sudden decline and disappearance of the whole civilisation. There are no signs of major violence from other peoples, no major invasions -- the Aryans arrived at a later time, archaeologists note. Floods or plagues might have contributed. But

> "...*in about 2000 B.C. the quality of the stone masonry became haphazard at Dholavira, indicating that the city was in decline ...The transportation system was disrupted. Trade must have fallen off. The easy wealth was no longer coming in. Eventually Dholavira was abandoned". "No one can say with certainty why the sub-continent's long-lived civilisation came to an end".*

By contrast, the beginnings of the civilisation seem to follow the same pattern of the rise of civilisations:

> "*Recent excavations prove that a village stood at Harappa's site in 3300 B.C., or 700 years before the advent of the city's great era, 2600 B.C.*". "*To archaeologists who dug in the first half of the 20th century, 'the Indus civilisation appears into being fully grown', as one wrote*".

Also historian Romila Thapar in her History of India points out that there had been a long period of slow evolution which gathered momentum towards the end and resulted in the spectacular Indus Valley Civilisation in c. 2300 B.C. The cities show evidence of an advanced sense of civic planning and organisation, and the presence of granaries suggest that there was a surplus produce that permitted city life and organisation. Then there was a decline, more a self decline as it seems, and rather rapid. We do not know whether it was influenced by the intrusion of less civilised peoples who occupied the sites of the Indus valley in the first half of the second millennium B.C. By 1700 B.C. the civilisation had already vanished before the coming of the Aryans.

During my recent visit to India I had the opportunity to read an interesting article on population problems of a particular kind: **Fertility is Power: Mother of all Paradoxes**, OUTLOOK, *The weekly Newsmagazine, March 8, 1999.*

I like the term **Paradoxes** on the very title: according to its Greek etymology it means *beyond the opinion, conflicting with expectation, a seemingly contradictory statement that may nonetheless be true.* I may add, against the general opinion we have on the topic of birth rates, of fertility, against the commonly accepted ideology in the Western countries as well as in developing countries in the world. The information from this article and the comments as a paradox are supportive of the notion that a high birth rate has a close relationship with progress in a wider sense, political progress first of all. My notion, however, includes the fact that creativity, that the genius of a people, of a civilisation, of an emerging social class within a civilisation, shows itself in the biological phase of a high birth rate, of fertility; and that it wanes in the other phase of low fertility up to the very death of that civilisation: maybe in a time that can be somewhat delayed from the climax of fertility, but clearly related to it.

Summarizing, the article states that in the most prosperous states in the south of India: Kerala, Tamil Nadu, but also Karnataka and Andhra Pradesh, the birth-rate is lower than in the northern ones: Uttar Pradesh, Bihar, Madhya Pradesh, Rajastan. The southern states are also more literate, and the campaigns in favour of family planning are more effective than in the north.

The problem arises from the fact that the distribution of the seats of the Parliament in Delhi is in proportion to the population of the particular states; and if the population grows in the North, where the control of the population growth is less effective than in the richer and more literate south, then in the near future the North will have more seats in Parliament, that is more political power. They are thinking of amending the Indian Constitution in order not to allow the South to lose today's proportion of representation, and political power. *"What is the point of curbing our family size if it is going to deprive us of political power? A situation that ... would have serious implications on India's crucial family planning programme."*

This may be the paradox of the ideology of family planning programmes.

Another important and well known publication in India, **Manorama, Yearbook 1999,** among other statistical data publishes an article (pag.460):

Religious Communities, Population by Religion, 1961 – 1991. Although the actual numbers change due to the general growth of the population, the percentage of the people adhering to the single religions shows something interesting to note. The Christians and the Jains from 2.4 % and 0.5 % in 1961 drop to 2.3 % and 0.4 % respectively. The Muslims from 10.7 % increase to 11.7 %; the Sikhs and the Buddhists from 1.8 % and 0.7 % to 2.0 % and 0.8 % respectively. The Hindus from 83.5 % drop to 82.4 %. Apart from the overwhelming and complex Hindu majority, the more educated Christians and Jains lose numbers and power in front of the less educated Muslims and Sikhs. Paradoxes of education, of family planning, and of general population problems.

This does not put an end to the comprehension of population problems according to the growth and the birth-rates. Much less to solve these problems. But at least it may shed some light in trying to better understand, against the too rational and materialistic ideology of the modern times. There were no such problems just a few centuries ago when we thought that the earth was large enough for all the peoples to expand. When dealing with populations, with human beings, with even a single man, there is always something we cannot grasp in full with our pure materialistic notions. We must question ourselves at least about the very reason of our being on this limited earth.

No serious economist today would say that an increase in the population in itself impedes the growth of the economy (Julian Simon and Bibek Debroy). A population may die of starvation due to natural disasters or to the malice of mankind but not due to an increase in the population itself. Starvation on a large scale can be caused by drought or, on a smaller scale when the father of the family is struck down with a heart attack just when his family needs him most. Again it can be brought about by man's malicious nature – when an enemy comes intentionally to do you harm, or when your own government leaders are thieves and corrupt: in Asia, in Africa, in Europe, today, always.

Ask any economist what it is that determines the growth of a country's GDP (Gross Domestic Product), and his reply will be: the land, the work force, its capital and the entrepreneurial spirit of the people. If we consider the work force as a factor associated with income, and the marginal product is not zero, the work force is not a negative influence. So, where is the problem if the population is high? Besides, the entrepreneurial spirit can do little without a work force and without technological improvements. Thomas Malthus based his theories on two premises:

1) The Earth has its limits and all its resources are likely to come to an end eventually. Malthus does not take into consideration that new resources are possible, that new natural resources may be discovered; nor does he take into consideration Man's creativity, his ingenuity and his genius.

A large part of the population can be considered useless inasmuch as it does not produce anything but it consumes the goods produced by others. If, therefore, this part of the population could be eliminated, the rest of the people would have more resources at their disposal. This could appear true today for those peoples in a phase of development inasmuch as they are unable to provide adequate instructions for an efficient social organisation and health services. Malthus made his catastrophic predictions shortly before the nineteenth century when the world population stood at fewer than a milliard. The neomalthusians today make the same catastrophic predictions as were made two centuries ago with a world population today of six thousand million inhabitants. There is more food available for every individual on Earth than there was two centuries ago.

THE RELATIONSHIP BETWEEN BIRTH RATES AND PROGRESS

In this essay my aim is to pursue the theories regarding the physical and mental evolution of mankind from his various anthropological stages: from Lucy to Neanderthal to the present-day homo sapiens. My more specific historical competence is in the history of the populations from ancient Greece and Rome to that of the Western world in both medieval and present times. This historical knowledge is not limited to history in the form of battles, wars and treaties; but it extends into linguistic, artistic, philosophic, religious and economic dimensions of our civilization---and of its internal transformations and spiritual evolutions. Unfortunately, my direct knowledge of non-European civilizations is somewhat limited regarding their present situation, their presence in the history of mankind and their physical and spiritual evolution.

Having studied the three-thousand-year course of the history of our ancient and modern western civilization, I have noticed certain human behavioural patterns and models of evolution which can be roughly compared to other civilizations outside of Europe and to the whole physical, somatic and spiritual evolution dealt with by anthropologists from the dawn of civilization to the present. In this essay I will keep in mind modern evolutionary theories, in particular that of the *cyclical rise and fall of human institutions* of the Italian philospher of history Giambattista Vico (1668-1744), including the evolution of a civilization with its internal formation of social classes. My opinions will be expressed using arguments that may go against or collide with the current conceptions of life in the western world as expressed, for example, by CNN and many institutions regarding population research.

My opinion or stand is the following:

humanity progresses when the birth rate is high; it does not progress, but regresses, when the birth rate is low, devolving towards its decadence and extinction.

In this context progress and regression do not mean happiness or sadness respectively, and the range of this phenomenon goes beyond the will of the individual, even beyond the will of those in power who could influence the behaviour of the masses in one way or the other. Today the governments of many countries tend to promote campaigns to limit their birth rates for various reasons which are often different and in antithesis with one another : the Earth cannot support too great a number of human beings, and the existing societies are unable to contain an excessive growth while at the same time try to program their social structures; in any case the positive economic standard of living obtained is to be maintained and not worsened. In the past (the recent past as well) we have had governments which, on the contrary, promoted demographic campaigns, often with imperialistic ends, as was the case with Fascism in Italy, or simply to survive as some governments are now doing in Europe.

Progress can certainly mean a larger availability of consumer goods--- refrigerators, automobiles, social services---but in particular this means growth towards a phase in which a social group, a civilization, or a country earns world fame politically, militarily, culturally and economically, creating arts, sciences, technology and better civil organizations, as well as consumer goods.

On looking at the demographic statistics of Great Britain in the last fifty years with its low demographic growth, and that of India (ex- colony politically subdued to Great Britain until 1947) with its high demographic growth, the acute observer is inclined to ask himself if it is conceivable today that Great Britain, or any other European country, could militarily, economically or even culturally subdue India. If European countries have progressed in a global sense (not just economically), in the last fifty years, India has showed an even greater increase and not only in the economic sense of the word *growth*. India has become a world power. The accurate statistics on the growth rate of these populations suggest some very interesting considerations, beyond those that the authors of the text *British Economic and Social History 1700-1975* (G. P. Hill, fourth edition (1977), Edward Arnold Publishers, 41 Bedford Square, London) are able to understand.

In 1707 England and Scotland had a population of about seven million inhabitants. In 1971 there were more than fifty-three million. In 1695 the estimate was around five and half million. Towards 1780 the growth began to become more rapid than in earlier epochs. In 1801 the population was of 10,500,000, in 1851 it was 20,800,000, in 1901 it was 37,000,000, in 1911 it was 40,830,000, in 1931 it was 44,800,000 and in 1971 the population was 53,874,000 inhabitants. It should be remembered that millions of inhabitants of the British Isles moved to America and to colonies of the once vast British Empire, and that a number by far inferior have been moving from the colonies of this long dismembered Empire to Great Britain in the last fifty years. Towards 1870 the birth rate starts to decline, with a decrease that becomes more and more accentuated as we near the present day. The birth rate was 3.63% in 1876 and 2.5% in 1911. The population continued to increase because the mortality rate decreased.

At the end of the 18th and early 19th centuries, contrary to the rest of the country, the areas near Birmingham and Manchester (centres of the Industrial Revolution) grow demographically; and that in the same period the increased production of foodstuffs and also the improvement of medical science contributed to this demographic increase: this is an interesting phenomenon that I consider almost secondary, although I must consider it in order to analyse the contemporary world. Another phenomenon which is interesting, although only secondary in importance, is urbanisation. A developing civilization manifests itself mainly, and above all, in its cities. The people who live in the country or in the farming districts move to the cities, thus increasing their population, and contributing to the economic and cultural development of the same cities which were already developing human environments. The phenomenon of emigration is similar to this: in the last two centuries the poorer European populations have found fortune by emigrating to the Americas and to the United States in particular. They found employment, they integrated into a new society which had already created organized civil institutions and which was a developing country. The coming of these new populations did not limit itself to increasing the population of the Americas but also enhanced this development.

The text under examination supplies us with other interesting details and the author asks himself the reason for this demographic revolution. Of the many general motivations suggested regarding this phenomenon in this text, the same author states that few are convincing. This is not a typically

British phenomenon because much the same thing has occurred in other countries with more or less similar characteristics. The change of climate and geography can be some of the factors---an induced phenomenon. Mysterious biological forces changed their virulence in epidemics; there can always be something biologically innate in the mutation of a growth rate in the population, and a period of stagnation can be followed by a livelier one. The author of the text underlines the fact that from 1750 to 1850 the real birth rate had increased, not only the number of adult living persons; and that later it progressively decreased until it reached a very low rate, a characteristic not limited to England alone but to all European countries, with some slight variations.

A general observation, which may be considered trivial, is that after a period of five hundred years in which England progressively organized itself into a modern state with its avantgard institutions, the 17th and 18th centuries are the moment in which it begins to affirm its supremacy by setting up colonies, by imposing its dominion on other peoples and thus building its Empire. It is the advent of the Industrial Revolution. A new social class is emerging: individuals from the lower classes are distinguishing themselves thanks to their human talents of intelligence and initiative. The men who invent and perfect the new machines in the factories and those who show a new spirit of enterprise belong to the lower, more humble classes. These men distinguish themselves from the others of the same class who remain humble and start asserting themselves only at a later date in history when the general tendency will be that of equality for all men. At first this equality is merely economic and obtained mainly by the intervention of the Labour party -- which is itself an institution produced by this tendency. The formation of this new social class with the Industrial Revolution and with this English dash towards colonization and the conquest of an Empire indicates a great period of progress of the English. This Anglo-Saxon progress is global, including military, political and economic progress, but more importantly, in this process of growth I think it important to underline progress in the form of the genius of the individuals who distinguished themselves in various fields of human activity. The text *British Economic and Social History, 1700-1975* states that after 1870 the birth rate has been decreasing slowly up to the present day. The parallel between the decreased birth rate and the decreased political and cultural prestige of England from the last century to present is immediately evident with the loss of its Empire and its scarce importance on the global stage. Despite the apparent splendour of the Victorian Age, historians assert that in 1837, the year in which Queen Victoria ascends to the throne of Great Britain, England had a greater political weight in the political spectrum of the world than it did in 1901, the year of her death. The contrary is true for India and other developing countries which have shown a high birth rate.

This consideration should be analysed with greater attention on the whole history of England in a European context from its Germanic tribes and their arrival to the British Isles and the formation of social classes: from Feudalism to the slow rise of the middle classes in the period that follows and finally the greater social equality of contemporary history. At this point it would be more opportune to state other, more general, examples of these phases of progress in other contexts in the history of the western world.

The birth rate of the Germanic tribes that invaded the Roman Empire after the 4th century A.D. was very high; in the end those same barbaric Germanic tribes imposed their dominion on the territories of this Empire, the same Empire which had earlier subdued and oppressed them. In his *Historia Longobardorum*, Paolo Diacono notes that the Longobard (Lombard) women had many children and that they showed a sense of superiority and contempt towards Roman women who were less prolific than they were. When they arrived in Italy in 558, their whole population was composed of 250,000 people---not very numerous if one considers the number of people in the territories that they were going to invade.

During the Republican era, which was the beginning of a period of demographic growth and conquest of the world, the birth rate of the Romans was very high. Roman women showed the same sense of moral superiority towards Etruscan women that the Longobard women would have shown centuries later: they were proud of their numerous offspring, they had confidence in their republic and contempt for the luxuries often associated with corruption.

The 19th century is the epos of the United States, with its conquest of the West and period of enormous progress in all fields of human activity. It was natural for the pioneer's wife to have numerous offspring; today it is less normal for the American family to have many children, and far less normal for the European family. It was difficult to raise a numerous family in the Far West with its bad living conditions, but this shows that children are not born only when the economic conditions of a family allow this: it is a natural primordial need that goes beyond the will of the couple or government. It is a sense of confidence in life on this earth, and eventually also in a religious dimension. This was a period of great expansion. Another consideration that could seem trivial, but is not, is that of the political and cultural weight of the United States today with its low birth rate and that of Russia (another Western country) with its relatively low birth rate if compared to its rate at the end of the Second World War. An alarming point emerges: despite all the possible implications that must be taken into consideration, neither the United States nor Russia were able to militarily subdue Vietnam or Afganistan respectively, the latter countries having a high demographic growth.

The same evolutionary pattern can be seen in the history of ancient Greece, during a period of more than a millenium, with numerous internal periods that can complicate one's understanding of this particular phenomenon, as is the case for all of modern western civilization. The more ancient periods were ones of growth and development, accompanied by an expansion which was not only political and economic: these were periods characterized by the manifestation of hellenic genius as well. In later periods of Roman conquest, there is the stagnation of Greek genius which is not as prominent as it was before, although in this period Greece maintains a high level of civilization which would later influence the whole ancient world in a positive way.

In Italy after the year 1000 A.D. and after centuries of decadence and ruin caused by barbaric invasions, there is a phase of exuberant growth: the civilization of the city-republics called **Comune** and of the maritime republics with their economic and spiritual explosion. The city-republics of Tuscany (the most famous of which is Dante Alighieri's medieval Florence) and those of the Po valley are preceded by (and continue contributing to) a conspicuous demographic growth. The scholar Villani, a contemporary of Dante, writes that in less than a century Florence's population soared from 9,000 to 100,000 inhabitants. At the end of the last century the Russian scientist Mendelev stated that if the high birth rate of Russia would remain so high for a long period of time, by the end of the 20th century Russia would have had between seven or eight hundred million inhabitants. The birth rate has obviously fallen since the end of the last century, and Russia has had some frightening calamaties that have hindered her growth rate from reaching the number predicted by this scientist. We cannot, however, deny that Russia has become one of the most powerful and prestigious countries in the world since the end of the last century. Hélène Carrère D'Encausse, in many French and American publications before 1980, states that in the Asiatic republics of the Soviet Union---usually Muslin republics---there is a high birth rate if compared to Russia, the same is true about other eastern Soviet republics. Despite the fact that these republics had a greater availability of consumer goods and foodstuffs if compared to Russia, this Franco-Russian author predicted the decadence and fall of this Empire to the advantage of these Asian provinces. It is surprising that nobody in America (where she has had her works published), as far as I know, has ever mentioned her name or quoted her works after the fall of the Soviet Union.

Therefore, a civilization or a new phase of a civilization begins with a biological need for a demographic growth in the form of an elevated birth rate. However, the opposite is true when a civilization has manifested itself during a rather long period of time: its birth rate decreases to the point where there is the loss of the vital impetus necessary for the continuity of a great civilization and the near disappearance or extinction of that same population. I believe that this theory goes beyond all other moral considerations. Another consideration to be made, which is closely linked to the phenomenon of an increased birth rate, is that in a social group whose growth rate is increasing, its sense of morality and religion is strengthened. Without linking this phenomenon to the birth rate as I have done, Vico would have stated that at a certain point in their evolution men create religions together with, or even before, creating a language, poetry or the civil institutions which characterize a primitive and barbaric humanity.

The Germanic tribes show a high birth rate before and during their migrations which in the Western world are called **barbaric invasions**. The Vikings who moved away from Scandinavia and the Arabs who expanded their presence in the Mediterranean show much the same characteristics. In the periods of expansion the Vikings, the Slavonic and Germanic peoples on one hand and the Arabs on the other can be considered civilizations at a different stage of internal evolution; but when they are in expansion they all demonstrate the same singular pattern of high birth rates. In fact, two thousand years before the expansion of the above-mentioned peoples, the Indo-European peoples had already begun migrating from northern India and Pamir towards the west, towards our Europe. The success in the following four thousand years of history, in some Middle-East populations, in ancient Greece and Rome and in modern Western Civilization, occurred in direct relation to their demographic growth, even in their eventual division in numerous nations which originated from only one ancient family. Some of these Indo-European nations were less fortunate. But it seems that the genius of a nation occurs in a dynamic evolving environment where there is also demographic growth.

Furthermore, a consideration which may seem the most trivial of all is that in this last century we have reached a very high level of social, scientific and economic progress that has no precedents in past epochs and that the world population today is more numerous than in past epochs. Even if we consider our history from 3000 B.C., during the formation of the first great Empires in Egypt and in the near east, we notice how progress in general is parallel to the growth of a nation in a particular geographical area. I believe those long periods preceding the above mentioned era should be defined as the biological evolution of the human species, rather than the evolution of a civilization. Those groups of human beings that do not sufficiently reproduce and do not, therefore, increase their presence on the Earth are destined to extinguish or disappear much in the same way other biological species do. It seems that the Neanderthals were a race of men that lived with other families of men who were more evolved biologically, in the end they ceased to exist much in the same way the branch of a family extinguishes. In time some groups are absorbed by other more vigorous groups. This is the case when a civilization reaches the last phase of its evolution and loses its vital impetus. The nations of a decadent Roman Empire are subdued by barbarians whose blood mingles with theirs, thus combining barbaric vigour with a superior culture and spiritual heredity which become the foundations of our modern Western Civilization.

The mortality rate must not be neglected. In the history of mankind there have been serious natural calamities like the pest, which in very little time decreased the world's population by a third, a half or maybe even more. If an epidemic kills a whole nation or even too big a part of it, we can no longer speak of progress with regards to this nation because death has erased life. These types of cases have occured in the history of mankind. In the jungles of Central America and in south east Asia there are ruins of cities whose existence seemed to have stopped suddenly and without an apparent reason: could an epidemic have killed all their inhabitants? In the case of the 14th century pest in Europe, an epoch of great progress and evolution towards a Rennaissance civilization, at least half the population survived, allowing it to continue its course towards greater progress.

A civilization develops in a period of time that is rather long, for Ancient Greece and the modern Western world this means at least ten centuries. Vico is the first to discuss **principles of ideal eternal history, in which all nations evolve in time with their rise, progress, states, decadence and fall.** In these **principles of ideal eternal history** I think that the pattern variation in the birth rate of a civilization should be included. Vico has paved the way towards a better understanding of the history of mankind organized in societies that evolve. His vision is modern, rational and almost materialistic, a vision in which man operates and suffers and questions himself on man's existence on this earth, finding an answer to his doubts in the Christian concept of Providence which operates inside and above the history of mankind.

The great parable of Greek and Roman civilization takes place according to the models we have mentioned but also in phases of lesser dimensions inside this parable. This is also true of modern Western Civilization, as we can see in the evolution of the social classes in England from William the Conqueror to the present day. The same phenomenon occurs in other historical contexts: in Italy, in Russia, in Athens during the era of Pericles, throughout Roman history from the Republic to the Empire, but the case of England seems more paradigmatic, more linear in its evolution.

In 1066 William of Normandy becomes William the Conqueror with his defeat of the Anglo-Saxons in the Battle of Hastings and gives his barons land in exchange for their services in this battle. His army is composed of about five thousand men and is a hierarchy composed of the king, barons and soldiers. The barons are soldiers that tower over the other soldiers because of their human value, and are recompensed with the distribution of the land and castles to a greater extent than are the mere soldiers and common people belonging to that same nation. William himself had demonstrated his value and political ability imposing his rule on Normans and Anglo-Saxons alike, guiding them intelligently and establishing an absolute monarchy: a monarchy that could be compared to the feudal-type monarchies of the homeric heroes. This type of feudal society was characterized by the presence of a king and feudal lords on one hand and by the oppressed common people in a subordinate position on the other. In another essay, *From Feudalism to Socialism*, I tried to show, step by step, how from an absolute monarchy the political institutions in England have had a tendency to evolve slowly and become more and more democratic. In the same context at the end of the cycle there is also the opposite tendency of centralizing power in the hands of political parties or governments who want to control economic initiative and the life of a nation itself. This essay does not limit itself to considering the relationship between birth rate and progress but also considers the evolution of social classes in England. This is a necessity as well, a primordial need that appears in all evolving civilizations. In the same way the physical and intellectual strength of the barons which at first was immense, with the passing of the centuries diminishes in their descendants although they enjoy the same privileges, and the same social prominence over those who they subdue. At the same time and from the same common people there are those who distinguish themselves for their merits, not necessarily the military merits of the first barons: the merchant class or bourgeoisie become richer and richer and begin having political importance. After the **Magna Carta** (1215) when the barons reunited in an attempt to control and limit the power of the absolute monarchy, in 1295 the commons (that is, the rich merchants who are not of noble lineage) unite in an assembly with the barons in the famous **Model Parliament**, and in 1341 the merchant class alone unites in the House of Commons: they are gradually destined to obtain more and more political power at the expense of nobles and barons who will lose almost all their political power at the turn of this century.

As far as political power is concerned the monarchy had lost a considerable amount with the Glorious Revolution of 1688 and in the next century. In the 16th century the Tudor kings favoured the middle classes rather than the nobility, and in the following century the political power belongs to the middle class. The 18th century is the triumph of the middle class. The lower classes, and the proletariat in particular, begin to make themselves heard and will have a political voice at a later date and after conflicts with the middle class. Throughout the history of England this slow evolution and tendency towards social and political equality among all men is perceivable, but becomes evident only with the Industrial Revolution. The bourgeoisie itself is subdivided into the upper middle class and the petite bourgeoisie, all common people who are a little more or a little less distinguished than the others until they obtain the ideal of equality for all men. It should be observed that every time a social class prepares to emerge, individuals of this class distinguish themselves from the others for some natural quality or merit; and this class shows a lively demographic increase. A social class in decline shows the opposite. In the case of the evolution from the Feudal class to the bourgeoisie to the proletarian class, these characteristics are not always so evident because of internal and induced phenomenon, whereas they appear very clearly when two civilizations are compared. In the 18th century, before the French Revolution, the distance between the social classes was more prominent in France than in England because of different political events, although we can consider it a parallel evolution. Both in France and England noble families are less prolific than the middle classes and the third class in general, and numerous documents show that noble families were not very concerned with the education of their offspring.

Another characteristic of a developing civilization or of an emerging social class together with a high birth rate is that strengthened moral and religious sense (not in the sense of orthodoxy) and a great degree of self-confidence.

The crusaders were part of the nobility that were distinguishing themselves from other European social classes, and Europe in general was giving signs of a new vitality with respect to other nations which were more culturally evolved. The English Puritans had irrational moral and religious stands yet they are the emerging middle classes, the Pilgrim Fathers of America and the founders of the Industrial Revolution in England. In north-east Italy at the end of the last century and in the first half of the 20th century the families of farmers were numerous and had a morally sound background. This lower social class with its tenacity and industriousness proved to be the foundation of the social and economic transformation of our epoch: progress and well-being.

In all three of these different social classes and European settings, families appear prolific, demonstrating trust in life and self-confidence and a high standard of moral behaviour that seems to decline in successive epochs. With the decline of a social class we have the decline of its birth rate, of its trust in life and manners and behaviour become more and more licentious. As far as the birth rate is concerned, besides the demographic decrease due to natural causes, to an innate need that manifests itself in a certain moment in history, we must keep in mind the induced phenomenon that can mislead one's understanding: the population could have increased due to better eating habits and food, better medical knowledge, in the same way it could have decreased due to birth control or medicine used to decrease births. At this point a moral consideration should be made: if we consider abortion a homicide at a personal level, it becomes a suicide at the social level or for a civilization as a whole. A country that promotes a campaign to limit births is as if it voluntarily wants to limit the development of the next generation in the sense of political predominance as well. It is as if it has lost confidence in life on this earth as well as in a religious dimension of an after life.

However, the problem of population and birth rate in the world remains a problem which is not completely understood and hence not resolved. The aim of this essay is not that of being a personal stand against birth control, as it may seem at a first glance, but that of illuminating the reader on this serious problem with different reasonings, this may be countercurrent, against the common opinion of politicians and men in general who neither have faith in life on Earth nor believe in a transcendent dimension of life. This essay goes against the views and theories of many American universities, against the concept of life that becomes ideology or idol to be adored and believed in, as was the case not long ago with Fascism or Socialism. An ideology that becomes an idol is a human creation rather like the arts and sciences: an ideology in which men believe.

One last point to make linked to growth, evolution and birth rate is that science and technology are made by man in an advanced phase of his evolution, a little before his last phase and of his inevitable devolution. In the case of a war of supremacy of one nation over another, it may occur that a nation surpasses another that possesses superior technology. In the case of the Romans, their technology was by far superior to that of the Germanic tribes who invaded them, not only regarding their civil works but also their armies and military skills, yet these barbarians occupied their Empire and subdued them. It must be remembered that these barbarians were open-minded and adopted some of the technological innovations of the superior Roman civilization, if not all of the spiritual inheritance of Roman civilization. Birth rate has already been discussed. In the era of the Persian wars, the Persians were heirs of a great civilization with a technology that was superior to that of the Greeks, yet the Greeks were in an evolutionary phase of expansion just before the age of Pericles and they conquered the Persians at Maratona and at Salamina, and then in the whole Persian Empire with the conquest of Alexander.

The Romans overtake the Etruscans first and Greece later towards 150 B.C., making the superior civilization of these nations their own. In both cases the Romans were in an initial phase of expansion with a high birth rate, and imbued with contempt towards the Etruscans and Greeks for their immorality.

With an inferior technology, yet ready to assimilate all that they can from the West even at the expense of many human lives, Vietnam and Afghanistan have brilliantly resisted American and Russian pressure. Arabs and Iranians, with inferior technology, with a very high---although irrational--moral sense stand up to America and the Western world in general. Khomeini showed contempt for the women of Paris and Western women in general, in a way which seems totally irrational to the Westerner. Iran and the Arab countries are more important on the world scene today than they were one or two generations ago, when their territories were subdued by European powers. The Puritans in England and America had an irrational behaviour as well but they were an emerging class that showed genius together with their irrationality, a genius that would allow their prevalence as nations.

Despite their inferior technology, and taking into consideration the help they had from Western countries, the Russians overtook the Germans in the Second World War. It may occur that a nation is defeated by another and that it is erased from the face of the Earth, when the differences are too evident, or that they are particularly unlucky. A nation can disappear because of natural causes---rather in the same way that the single individual cannot mature and grow simply because he dies at an early age.

When I study the history of past centuries, or when we discuss the current political situation of my country or of the contemporary world in general, although I consider economic, political and cultural factors, I also take into consideration the birth rate of a particular nation with anthropological intentions rather than moral ones. It sometimes happens that I am able to give a more or less correct hypothesis on what will happen in the near future, which was the case when I anticipated the transformation of Russia from a dictatorship to a nation with more democratic forms of government and with less political prestige. This was done simply by analysing the models of evolution of English and French political institutions, comparing them to the institutions present in Russian history and keeping in mind the variable birth rate factor in all these countries. If I were to search for a person of genius in the history of a nation, I would know where to look: if he were a poet or the founder of a religious institution I would look for him in a primitive period or the beginning of a civilization, in one of its internal phases or in a simple social class. If I were to search for a world-famous scientist or simply an intelligent factory worker that builds or perfects a new machine, I would look for him in a more mature or less primitive environment or setting. My search would be like that of the geologist who looks for diamonds (or oil) in particular environments according to his knowledge of the Earth and the intuition of a thinking being.

ARCHAEOLOGY AND POPULATION GROWTH

It is commonly said that population started to grow enormously when agriculture was invented. This happened independently in several parts of the world and at different historical times: in the Near East and Egypt first but also in the Indus Valley, in South East Asia, in northern China, in north-eastern America, in Meso America and South America. It is also said that wheat and barley, the first important crops, could be easily cultivated in Europe, in the Near East, while this is not true for the region south of the Sahara: this would be the reason why one does not see a similar pattern of agricultural or population explosion into this area in neolithic times: I do not agree with this last statement as the reason for me lies rather with the very fact of the evolution and maturation of a people, of a civilisation, more than with the environmental conditions which could also be very important; and also in the longer times of the evolution of man, in the growing capacity of the human skull to contain the brain, in the capacity of man to think in abstract, to understand mathematics and create technology. If the invention of agriculture allowed more people to be fed, if it contributed to the growth in the number of these people, let us put it the other way – at least tentatively: the progress of mankind was basically created just in a phase of growing population of a particular group of people. The agricultural advance, which is the creation of new technology in this particular moment of human history, in turn permitted a growth of the population as a side effect, an induced phenomenon. Not even Prof. Luigi Luca Cavalli Sforza with his otherwise brilliant studies in anthropology and population problems seems to be aware of this particular aspect of civilisations.

There is plenty of circumstantial evidence to support the thesis that it was the evolution and the maturation of a civilisation to create organised agriculture, and progress in the broader sense, in the Middle East, in Ancient Mesopotamia, in the Sumerian Civilisation. The Sumerian civilisation lasted some thirteen hundred years (roughly from 3300 to 2000 BC), the same length of time as Western civilisation from the barbaric invasions of our Middle Ages to the present day, the same as the Roman and Greek civilisations.

Scholars are still divided about when the Sumerians – that is those who spoke the language later called Sumerian – arrived in the area: they may have been there since about 4000 BC. But since we know the population of civilised Sumerians to be a mixture of races, perhaps including the earlier inhabitants of the region, with a culture which mixed foreign and local elements, this is not important for this kind of research. But only in this relatively small area in the region where the rivers Tigris and Euphrates meet did a pattern of village life common to much of the Near East begin to grow faster and harden into something else. From that background emerges the first true urbanism, a better organised society, that of Sumer, and the first observable civilisation.

Together with the invention of agriculture with the construction of canals for irrigation there was the invention of writing. Both inventions were progressively improved and perfected. From the general information at my disposal in history books and anthropologic essays, I have the impression that these people gathered technical and scientific information from other older civilisations in the area and re-elaborated them. This is a pattern of the phenomenon of transculturalisation. They perfected them and added something new – which is the legacy of their genius. But this part came in a later period of their history, in a later phase of the evolution of their civilisation, in a period when they were more rational, before they were annexed and assimilated into other new civilisations, mainly Semitic peoples but also Indo-Europeans. They used cuneiform writing for practical uses, for communication, for consultation of records. It strengthened government organisation and made the exploitation of resources more efficient. Writing, organised agriculture and the observation of the stars reflect more a rational and scientific attitude rather than an emotional and poetic or religious one. When their civilisation was about to wane and pass its legacy to younger and more aggressive civilisations, transculturalisation – a message from one civilisation to another, the legacy of the human conquests to be passed to and used by another civilisation -- showed an interesting pattern which would repeat itself dramatically in other epochs and with other civilisations in different times, including our very present epoch. Writing and the language on one part and the knowledge of the stars on the other became more emotional: the basis for religious beliefs, for epic poems, for the creation of myths and of great poetry. Science and technology are culture, like poetry in preceding epochs. Both are things created by man. Modern science and technology have been created mainly by Europeans, by Westerners. (Let us forget for the moment, for this kind of research, the enormous contributions that other civilisations brought to science and technology and that were passed on to the West, to Europe – the very same phenomenon of transculturisation in other times and in another direction.) The Japanese, the Indians, the Chinese, in contact with the Westerners, absorb this kind of culture – modern science and technology, they make it their own, they may even go beyond and surpass the whole Western Civilisation in the near future, both in science and technology on one part and political prestige and supremacy on the other. To note also that these Asian peoples, independently from one another, were in that phase of their maturation that they were ready to pick up the legacy of the European civilisation. Or also, the West may even wane and almost disappear from the face of the earth because of the low birth rates and the loss of their vital driving force.

Much that is known of the Upper Palaeolithic confirms the sense that the crucial genetic changes are behind and that the evolution is now a mental and social phenomenon. The distribution of major racial divisions in the world which last down to early modern times is already broadly fixed by the end of the Upper Palaeolithic. Geographical and climatic divisions had produced specialisations within Homo Sapiens in skin pigment, hair characteristics, the shape of the skull and the bone structure of the face. In the earliest Chinese relics of Homo Sapiens the Mongoloid characteristics are discernible. All the main racial groups are established by 10,000 BC, broadly speaking in the areas they dominated until the resettlements of the Indo-Europeans which was one aspect of the rise of the European civilisation to world domination after 1500 AD. The Upper Palaeolithic world was still a very empty place by modern standards. Calculations suggest that twenty thousand humans lived in France in Neanderthal times, possibly fifty thousand years ago. There were perhaps ten million humans in the whole world, living mainly by hunting and gathering. Cultural changes and progress were necessarily slow. Although there is still much unknown about the groups that lived in Upper Palaeolithic times in southern France and in central Europe in general -- those who made the magnificent cave paintings, there are two important things to notice: they were both larger in size than in former times, and also more settled and organized. Second, there was a sudden end for this civilisation. The impression left by the violence of the contrasts between what was before and what came after produces a sense of shock. So relatively sudden an extinction is a mystery. We have no precise dates or even precise sequences. Nothing ended in one year or another: there was only a gradual closing down of artistic activity over a long time which seems in the end to have been absolute. Some scholars have blamed climate and changing environment.

The changing of the environment must always and in any case be taken into consideration. But let us put it again in another perspective. Civilisations rise and fall according to rather precise patterns of evolution, including high and low birth rates, and the disappearance of a civilisation. There are many other examples of civilisations which rose and fell by themselves almost following an internal biological need of growing to preponderance and of waning in the end. There are civilisations of which we know everything, and other civilisations of which we know very little, or nothing at all. Archaeologists in recent years have been of great help in understanding civilisations which were unknown, or adding information and knowledge to civilisations we already know. Anthropologists are helpful too.

As a humanist with a cultural formation in the field of languages, of history, of philosophy of history, interested in man in a comprehensive way that evolves as a biological species and creates arts sciences and human institutions, I see interesting parallels in the civilisations I think I know -- with other civilisations present in the world today, and civilisations in past epochs, in historic and prehistoric times: I feel sure enough to think that I can contribute to comprehend the reason of man's presence in this world: patterns of evolution I have observed in epochs and in civilisations I am acquainted with can tentatively be applied to other epochs and civilisations in order to better understand them – as if it were a mathematical calculus of probability.

Progress in the broader sense I mean in these essays was very slow during the long millennia of human evolution. It was accelerated in proportion to the growth of the people in the whole world in general, and in the moment of the growth of a social group, of a civilisation in particular. Some civilisations simply disappeared for reasons we do not fully understand, and also some human races disappeared: we do not know how and why. The Neanderthals disappeared after having lived a long time together with other humans of other species of homo sapiens. Other hominids disappeared we do not know how and whether they left any legacy. Other human groups, let us call them human species, are very weak today and on the brink of disappearing from the face of the earth like other biological species of the animal and vegetal world: this may be because of natural reasons or also because of the aggressive presence and greed of civilised man which considers himself superior. In historical times the Romans in their conquests, for one example, annihilated entire peoples and absorbed some of them. Other smaller peoples were annexed and absorbed culturally and physically by greater civilisations, by more prestigious cultural and political states, by cultural centres.

Other human races may be physically strong, not at all on the verge of extinction, but may not yet be ready to pick up the message of the moribund Western Civilisation: its science, its technology, its rational way of thinking and political organising. We do not know what will happen to them in the long run. The Aborigines of Australia have been able to create arts and myths according to the very same pattern other civilisations had done when they were in a primitive stage: the myths of the Aborigines can be compared to the myths of the Greeks, and of other civilisations. The myths of the Germanic tribes in Roman times can also be compared to the myths of the Greeks. Through myths first and more rational behaviour in more mature times, we can understand the distinct personality of each people, of each civilisation. We can feel the essence of their personality from their legacy, through the arts and sciences they have left – in a similar way as we feel the personality of single persons who live near us and with whom we are in contact everyday.

The populations south of the Sahara might grow and evolve and dominate the earth the way the Westerners have done and the Asians seem to be going to do. Then, when this happens, maybe in the distant future when the others have disappeared -- they may feel an interest in modern day civilisations in a way that recalls how we modern Europeans are interested today in primitive civilisations of past millennia. In any case they count in the world today, culturally and even politically, more than they did one century ago or a few centuries ago. Racism on the part of the Westerners or the Asians may be today one aspect of that sense of superiority the strong man feels against the weaker one: the pride and the prejudice of those who belong to the winning side of history may feel against the vanquished. It is also possible that all men and all civilisations together disappear from the face of the earth, like other biological species, either for natural biological causes or also man made, – not to mention the end of the world in religious terms.

In the Gilgamesh Epic men seem to be irreverent to the gods: they have won their commandments by constructing canals – men can live with their own power and intelligence, without depending on the whims of the gods. They seem modern men who have confidence in science and do not need religion, they do not need God. This epic is more complex of course, and reflects other positions as well. The Sumerians notice that the lambs are born in the spring when the stars are in a certain position. This is rational scientific observation for them. Later on, more primitive people in the same geographical area but in another phase of their evolution, take this new piece of information as religious, as an influence of Jupiter and the other stars on the birth of the lambs at a certain astronomical conjunction in the spring. And they make gods of the stars.

Men create religions, said Vico. Man created God, not the other way, said Feuerbach one century later. This was said also by some rational philosophers in ancient times both in India and in Greece in the hellenistic period. This is another pattern which would repeat itself in history again, from one cultural environment to another.

National Geographic is not happy with my notion of the relationship between birth – rates and progress. The same can be said of many people of institutes in America and in the world concerned with population problems. Interestingly enough, a few people are worried about my position, many others are definitely against it without even taking it into consideration, maybe because their ideology blinds them and prevents their understanding.

In the issue of December 1999 *National Geographic* published an interesting essay on the Greeks, focussed on the heroic age. It made me feel the same emotions I felt at the age of 16 when I had to read one book of the *Iliad* in the original Homeric dialect - which was easier to understand for us young students than the prose of, say, historian Tukydides. Not having continued practicing this, now I have forgotten the language. The map, the stress on the various periods from the Mycenaeans onward, and many pieces of information were great. Now I can better understand why the heroes prayed the gods for good favourable winds, the reason for the shape of their shields, and the fact that the Trojans were Luvians.

There is another topic that I would like to link to this one of the Greeks, that is (over)population problems, and paradoxes, of which two interesting essays have been recently published by *National Geographic*, and more are to be published. In those two essays everything was proper and correct, but I would like to shed some light in order to understand the problem from another perspective, as a complication to the problem – which always happens when the lives of human beings are in question. Civilisation progresses (economically, in political prestige, in the arts, the sciences and technology), when the birth rate is high. On the contrary there is no progress for that civilisation, there is death and no future on the earth for them, when the birth rate is low. That is the final stage of the evolution of a civilisation – before dying out or before being overcome by other more barbarian civilisations that are in the expanding phase. Both high and low birth rates are normal phenomena (as are also high and low moral standards). *National Geographic* does not seem to be willing to accept such a notion, like most American universities.

On page 75 the essay states:

> "*The collapse of the Mycenaean world…..a period of shrinking populations, poverty, and cultural decline….*"

Bingo! We are approaching this very stage now in Europe.

This is a pattern I noticed in dozens of other historical contexts, together with other patterns such as moral decadence, or moral reinforcement with irrational manifestations, creation of technology more than in preceding periods. By contrast, when the Greeks expanded all over the Mediterranean sea like "*frogs around the pond*", that was a phase of growth and expansion, and of progress for them in more extensive terms. The *Iliad* and the *Odyssey* are artistic (poetic) products at the very beginning of this second phase, of a new civilisation, even if the spiritual legacy of the Mycenaeans on them and of all previous civilisations is evident to us. In the same way, Dante belongs to the modern western civilisation – with positive influences from the ancient western civilisation.

Now we in the West, more so in Europe than in America, with all our splendid civilisation, can consider ourselves at the evolutionary level of the Mycenaeans around 1100 BC with their "*shrinking populations*", before their own fall, for biological reasons. No matter if other causes could have contributed such as earthquakes, plagues, "*marauding sea people*" or "*migrating Dorians*": such as migrating Germanic tribes all over Europe and the Roman Empire almost two millennia later, or migrating Aryans into India over-imposing previous civilisations. It does not matter if in the West today the shrinking populations can be caused, in addition to natural causes, also by man-made medical techniques that help reduce fertility and birth rates. I see us in the West now in the very same position of the Mycenaeans around 1100 BC before their fall, before the end of their cycle: other peoples may take advantage of our culture, of our science and technology – Chinese, Indians, Arabs. It is just possible that they conquer us militarily, they may annihilate us, or without such catastrophes, they simply might take our place as we are going to diminish our presence in the world or also disappear from the face of the earth because our vital driving force has vanished.

As for the pattern of declining birth-rates and morals, this is what Plutarch wrote at the beginning of the second century AD regarding the decline of the Greek civilisation:

> "*One remarks nowadays all over Greece such a low birth rate and in general manner such depopulation that the towns are deserted and the fields lying fallow, although this country has not been ravaged by war or epidemic. The cause of this harm is*

evident. By avarice or by cowardice, the people, if they marry, will not bring up children that they ought to have. At most, they bring up one or two ..... It is in this manner that the scourge, before it is noticed, has rapidly developed. The remedy is in ourselves, we have but to change morals."

Despite Plutarch's exhortations, the ancient Greeks didn't change their morals, and so died out (information from Jacqueline Kasun, *P.R.I. Review*, 2000). The history of the Greek civilisation is well known to us, with its internal phases which match those of modern Europe and of the Western civilisation in general, including this interesting phenomenon of the variation of the birth rates.

National Geographic published another interesting article on the Indus Valley Civilisation (June 2000). There is not as much evidence regarding the Harappa civilisation as there is for the civilisations of Egypt and Mesopotamia, as we have not yet been able to decipher their writing. Yet scholars and archaeologists are puzzled at the fact of the sudden decline and disappearance of the whole civilisation. There are no signs of major violence from other peoples, no major invasions -- the Aryans arrived at a later time, archaeologists note. Floods or plagues might have contributed. But

> *"...in about 2000 B.C. the quality of the stone masonry became haphazard at Dholavira, indicating that the city was in decline ...The transportation system was disrupted. Trade must have fallen off. The easy wealth was no longer coming in. Eventually Dholavira was abandoned". "No one can say with certainty why the sub-continent's long-lived civilisation came to an end".*

By contrast, the beginnings of the civilisation seem to follow the same pattern of the rise of civilisations:

> *"Recent excavations prove that a village stood at Harappa's site in 3300 B.C., or 700 years before the advent of the city's great era, 2600 B.C.". "To archaeologists who dug in the first half of*

the 20th century, 'the Indus civilisation appears into being fully grown', as one wrote".

Also historian Romila Thapar in her History of India points out that there had been a long period of slow evolution which gathered momentum towards the end and resulted in the spectacular Indus Valley Civilisation in c. 2300 B.C. The cities show evidence of an advanced sense of civic planning and organisation, and the presence of granaries suggest that there was a surplus produce that permitted city life and organisation. Then there was a decline, more a self decline as it seems, and rather rapid. We do not know whether it was influenced by the intrusion of less civilised peoples who occupied the sites of the Indus valley in the first half of the second millennium B.C. By 1700 B.C. the civilisation had already vanished before the coming of the Aryans.

National Geographic, August 2000, also gives some interesting information on the civilisation that left the temples of Angkor in the jungle of Cambodia: I would like to read it according to my own ideology and to my own patterns of evolution.

> "*The Tonle Sap was to the Khmer what the Nile was to the ancient Egyptians.... The Khmer learned to divert the retreating water to increase rice production. As the population increased, the Khmer began to manage water ever more intensively, not only for agriculture but also for religious purposes. ... Such works required centralized planning and the hand of an absolute ruler – the god-king. The resulting rice surpluses freed labor for other uses, notably constructing the god-king's temples. ... In the 12th century the capital of Angkor may have embraced a population of one million. By comparison Paris, one of the great cities in Europe at the time, had a population of perhaps 30,000. ... (King) Jayavarman died mysteriously around 1220, and the Angkor civilisation went into decline. The last stone temple at Angkor was built around 1290. Around 1430 Siam invaded from west, and the fleeing Khmer abandoned Angkor, eventually establishing a new capital at Phnom Penh...."*

From these essays of *National Geographic* there are no direct statements, there is no direct information that there was a rise and fall of birth rates, of fertility, but they seem to me rather clearly implied as circumstantial evidence that in the beginning there was almost an explosion of the population, and that at the end the populations shrank, lost their vital driving force, and almost disappeared on their own without external causes.

The Vikings also seem to have undergone the same pattern -- an increase in the fertility of their populations in the times preceding their migrations, their raids into western Europe, the Mediterranean sea and central Russia. (*National Geographic, In Search of Vikings, May 2000*).

The series of articles of National Geographic addressing population are well balanced, much better than articles on similar topics in other magazines (*National Geographic, October 1998: Human Migration, Women and Population, Feeding the Planet*).

An article from *Scientific American December 2000, Paleolitic Pit Stop*, also gives some interesting hints. Author Kate Wong suggests that Neanderthals and early modern humans behaved similarly at a French site, which may be interesting enough for its own sake. Author Wong is interested especially in the slow technological progress of early humans in those caves in southern France – the oldest best preserved fireplaces which date between 54,000 and 66,000 years ago.

> "Although a radical shift did not occur between the Middle and Upper Paleolithic, Simek notes that significant change did come later with the so-called Magdalenian period, perhaps because population size was increasing. Remains from sediments toward the back of the cave reveal that around 12,500 years ago the Magdalenians used Grotte XVI specifically as a hunting site, leaving behind characteristic harpoons and other implements...."

There certainly is a population problem – how to feed the planet, how to go on living in an environment that we contribute to spoil. The fact that technology has helped us to feed more people is promising: it proved Thomas Malthus almost wrong in his gloomy anticipations two centuries ago, but it does not assure us much for the life and well being of the future generations. After two centuries of progress and of population explosion, today we seem to be at the very same time and at the very same position of Thomas Malthus, with the same worries for our future.

Why does *National Geographic* not put the entire problem from another point of view as well, not only a positivistic and rational one, but also question the reason of the very presence of man on the earth? Why not consider populations and civilisations, expanding and shrinking, as living entities different from the single individuals that make them up? They seem to have their own internal biological laws which reflect more or less the same pattern of growth, evolution, maturity, decadence and fall, like other biological species living in larger groups. Unlike other biological species, civilisations progress, create new technology, sometimes they learn and use technology made by other civilisations – that is somewhat the legacy from other civilisations, or leave it to other civilisations. Sometimes this legacy is completely lost, or at least this is what we are inclined to think when we find the remnants of other civilisations in archaeological excavations and we are puzzled and wondered by their achievements of many centuries ago.

Interestingly enough, the most extreme religious denominations such as the Catholic Church and the Muslims are those who have more confidence in the future of man on this earth as they have faith and confidence in God and in man in a religious dimension, both in the earthly and especially in eternal life. Instead, those who have confidence in themselves on this earth only, in their abilities and in their reason only, after a period of self confidence excessive pride and excitement --show less confidence in their future and in themselves.

I would also question: what is progress? Why is there progress? Does it do anything good for me in addition to providing a better material life? Is there a God and does he factually intervene in the history of men as Providence? And how? Someone suggested to me that "progress" is directly linked to sin – the original sin and the sins of men on this earth.

THE TASMANIANS

We have already seen how a high birth rate is in direct relation to scientific, technological and economic progress, and to the political assertion of one certain social group or culture. On the contrary, a low birth rate is associated with the loss of such progress. The Roman Empire began to manifest a low birth rate in the last centuries of its dominance, in the third and fourth centuries A. D. and the population decreased throughout the whole of Europe. Also the economic level of life diminished, technological knowledge was lost, not only in Roman Britain but in all the territories of the Empire. The Romans had constructed buildings, roads, bridges, ships. The technology used for the building of bridges, roads and Roman ships would only be surpassed more than a thousand years later with the invention of the steam engine, with the new modern Western culture, with a new lively increase of the population.

Another case in which a cultural group manifests a loss of its technical and scientific knowledge in the passage of time, in a completely different environment, was published in articles in the *National Geographic Magazine* (April 2005) and the *Scientific American* (*The Morning of the Modern Mind*, by Kate Wong, June 2005) regarding the Aborigenes of Tasmania and Australia and other populations in Africa and Asia about 50,000 years ago, in the medio-paleolithic period. In the 19th century the English killed all the native aborigines of Tasmania, about a few thousand, therefore these native aborigines no longer exist. The Tasmanians who are now extinct used roughly chipped stones as tools, they didn't possess bows and arrows, they didn't know how to fish and they didn't know how to light a fire.

*   *   *

Tools from Blombos (South Africa) are more sophisticated than those typically found at Middle Stone Age sites. The bone implements include awls worked to a fine point and polished with ochre to achieve a smooth patina.....

Population growth. *Modern ways bubbled up and disappeared at different places until the population size reached critical mass. At that point, confrontation between groups and competition for resources sparked symbolic behavior and spurred technological innovation, contend researchers, including Alison Brooks of George Washington University and Sally McBrearty of he University of Connecticut. And with more people to pass on these traditions, they began to stick, rather than dying out with the last member of a group.*

The circumstances most likely to elicit advanced cultural behaviors, McBrearty and others hypothesize, were those related to increased population size. The presence of more people put more pressure on resources, forcing our ancestors to devise cleverer ways to obtain food and materials for toolmaking, she submits. More people also raised the chances of encounters among groups. Beads, body paint and even stylised tool manufacture may have functioned as indicators of an individual's membership and status in a clan, which would have been especially important when laying claim to resources in short supply. ...

.....Conversely, when the population dwindled, these advanced practices subsided – perhaps because the people who engaged in them died out or because in the absence of competition they simply did not pay off and were therefore forgotten. The Tasmanians provide a recent example of this relationship: when the Europeans arrived in the region in the 17th century, they encountered a people whose material culture was simpler even than those of the Middle Paleolithic, consisting of little more than basic stone flake tools. Indeed, from an archaeological standpoint, these remains would have failed to nearly all tests of modernity that are commonly applied to prehistoric sites. Yet the record shows that several thousand years ago, the Tasmanians possessed a much more complex tool kit, one that included bone tools, fishing nets, and bows and arrows. It seems that early Tasmanians had all the latest gadgetry before rising sea levels cut the island off from the mainland 10,000 years ago but lost the technology over the course of their small group's separation from much larger Aboriginal Australian population.

This might be why South African sites between 60,000 and 30,000 years old so rarely seem to bear the modern signature: demographic reconstruction suggests that the human population in Africa crashed around 60,000 years ago because of a precipitous drop in temperature. Inferring capacity from what people produced is inherently problematic, White observes. Medieval folks doubtless had the brainpower to go to the moon, he notes......

Controversial evidence from the rock shelters of Malakunanja II and Nauwalabila I in Australia's Northern Territory, for instance, suggests that people had arrived there by 60,000 years ago. To reach the island continent, emigrants travelling from southeastern Asia would have to have built sturdy watercraft and navigated a minimum of 50 miles of open water, depending on the sea level. Scholars mostly agree that any human capable of managing this feat must have been fully modern.

And in Israel's Qafzeh Cave, Erella Hovers of the Hebrew University of Jerusalem and her team recovered dozens of pieces of red ochre near 92,000-year-old graves of H. sapiens.....

(Scientific American, *June 2005, The Morning of the Modern Mind, by Kate Wong)*

In the opinion of Kate Wong, stated in her long article about similar cases, men can also lose their technical knowledge with the passing of time for various reasons. The first reason could be the isolation of a limited group caused by changes of climate and environment and mention is made of the stagnation or decrease in the population in periods of time more or less notable. The rather lengthy isolation of a population could also lead to another phenomenon: a reduction in size of their individuals, which seems to have happened on the island of Flores, or the opposite phenomenon of a growth in size as has happened for some other biological species. The author, however, makes numerous references to growth in population in relation to a phase of technological progress: improved agriculture for example can sustain a more numerous population (an important fact which I however retain to be in some way induced). Kate Wong of the Scientific American does not want, however, to underline the fact that just this increase in the population could be one of the factors underlying the expression of the creative genius of a population – even if maximum caution should be used when considering populations so distant from us. Caution both in formulating hypotheses and in trusting the archaeological data in our possession.

The Tasmanians had probably lost their technological knowledge after reaching the new lands of the Australian continent at least ten thousand years ago, no longer being able to light a fire and construct arms and material objects, things which the inhabitants of the continent in the 18th century were still able to do. In a similar way, the aborigines of the continent probably lost the technical knowledge of navigation they possessed when they crossed the Straits of Torres and navigated the seas around the other islands of the Indonesian Archipelago in vessels relatively advanced 40 or 50 thousand years ago. In this long period of time the Tasmanians and the Australian aborigines have shown a population increase which is relatively lower than that shown by other populations both in Europe and in Asia, populations which have reached levels of civilization with more advanced technology. Also the aborigines of the Andaman in the Indian Ocean are few in number, a few hundred individuals. Other primitive societies observed, in isolated localities in the Indonesian Archipelago, in the Philippines, in Australia, in South America and in Africa also resulted numerically insignificant, in spite of maintaining a strong sense of the individuality and the personality of their particular culture. In 50,000 years, having crossed the Straits of South-East Asia, they have not developed great cultural societies compared to those of North Africa, South Asia, the Middle East, Mesoamerica, of China and of Europe. It seems just as though they have lost the technical and scientific knowledge they possessed earlier. And they have not grown in number to reach the hundreds of millions of human presences on their territory, as has happened for the other civilizations of the Middle East, of Asia and of Europe, for the Semites, for the Indoeuropeans, for the Mongols, before our actual epoch.

PARADOXES

During my recent visit to India I had the opportunity to read an interesting article on population problems of a particular kind: **Fertility is Power: Mother of all Paradoxes**, OUTLOOK, *The weekly Newsmagazine, March 8, 1999.*

I like the term **Paradoxes** on the very title: according to its Greek etymology it means *beyond the opinion, conflicting with expectation, a seemingly contradictory statement that may nonetheless be true.* I may add, against the general opinion we have on the topic of birth rates, of fertility, against the commonly accepted ideology in the Western countries as well as in developing countries in the world. The information from this article and the comments as a paradox are supportive of the notion that a high birth rate has a close relationship with progress in a wider sense, political progress first of all. My notion, however, includes the fact that creativity, that the genius of a people, of a civilisation, of an emerging social class within a civilisation, shows itself in the biological phase of a high birth rate, of fertility; and that it wanes in the other phase of low fertility up to the very death of that civilisation: maybe in a time that can be somewhat delayed from the climax of fertility, but clearly related to it.

Summarizing, the article states that in the most prosperous states in the south of India: Kerala, Tamil Nadu, but also Karnataka and Andhra Pradesh, the birth-rate is lower than in the northern ones: Uttar Pradesh, Bihar, Madhya Pradesh, Rajastan. The southern states are also more literate, and the campaigns in favour of family planning are more effective than in the north.

The problem arises from the fact that the distribution of the seats of the Parliament in Delhi is in proportion to the population of the particular states; and if the population grows in the North, where the control of the population growth is less effective than in the richer and more literate south, then in the near future the North will have more seats in Parliament, that is more political power. They are thinking of amending the Indian

Constitution in order not to allow the South to lose today's proportion of representation, and political power. *"What is the point of curbing our family size if it is going to deprive us of political power? A situation that ... would have serious implications on India's crucial family planning programme."*

This may be the paradox of the ideology of family planning programmes.

Another important and well known publication in India, **Manorama, Yearbook 1999,** among other statistical data publishes an article (pag.460): **Religious Communities, Population by Religion, 1961 – 1991.** Although the actual numbers change due to the general growth of the population, the percentage of the people adhering to the single religions shows something interesting to note. The Christians and the Jains from 2.4 % and 0.5 % in 1961 drop to 2.3 % and 0.4 % respectively. The Muslims from 10.7 % increase to 11.7 %; the Sikh s and the Buddhists from 1.8 % and 0.7 % to 2.0 % and 0.8 % respectively. The Hindus from 83.5 % drop to 82.4 %. Apart from the overwhelming and complex Hindu majority, the more educated Christians and Jains lose numbers and power in front of the less educated Muslims and Sikhs. Paradoxes of education, of family planning, and of general population problems.

This does not put an end to the comprehension of population problems according to the growth and the birth-rates. Much less to solve these problems. But al least it may shed some light in trying to better understand, against the too rational and materialistic ideology of the modern times. There were no such problems just a few centuries ago when we thought that the earth was large enough for all the peoples to expand. When dealing with populations, with human beings, with even a single man, there is always something we cannot grasp in full with our pure materialistic notions. We must question ourselves at least about the very reason of our being on this limited earth.

Another interesting observation on the population of India. Indian magazines but also American media such as *Time* and *Newsweek* report some statistical projections on the economy: by the year 2010 the GNP of India should reach and equal the GNP of England France and Italy, if the current growth is steady and if there are no crisis such as the recent one in the south east of Asia, or if no major political problems occur. However, they say that the wealth of the nation, of India, is being produced by only a percentage of the whole population, say by one hundred or one hundred fifty million people – the most active part of the population, while the others contribute little and are only a burden which causes problems. A comment: would India be a great country, a world power, if the population were only one hundred and fifty million with a GNP comparable to Britain's?

The same can be said for China. They anticipate that by the year 2020 the per capita income of the Chinese should reach the level of South Korea if the actual economic trends are kept constant with no major setbacks, which is always possible. In the meantime South Korea and the other countries would go on and progress on their own, of course. In this case the GNP of China would simply be almost the double of the GNP of the U S A today. The consequences would be great – greater than the consequences on a world wide scale caused by the restructuring of the Soviet Union after 1989. Consequences that affect a civilisation, not only an era. The West, and Europe in particular, would shy away and feel weak, like a single old person that retires in good order in front of aggressive younger people and prepares to die, leaving the world to others, to other people of a different family.

There are six billion people in the world today, and we are worried that the food supply is not sufficient for everybody. Still there seems to be more food today for every single person even in the poorest countries than a generation ago, or one century ago. This is not to deny that there is a problem, this is only to notice the paradox: there is more food, there has been progress in the world even with an exploding population.

By 1800, two centuries ago, Thomas Malthus was worried about the growth of the population, in the very middle of the industrial revolution in England. The conditions of the lower classes, of the workers in the factories, of the so called proletariat, remind us of the conditions of the poor in India. But his worries were the very same as the worries today in times of economic expansion, and nationalism, in Asia. Yet the world population at that time was under one billion.

The Germanic tribes that were leaving their regions to invade the territories of the Roman Empire in the fifth and sixth centuries AD, in addition to other causes, were leaving their regions because the forests were depleted, there were too many people in the regions of northern Europe. The land could not sustain them.

If you are a doctor, a nurse, a man or a woman of good will concerned with the life and wellbeing of your family on this earth; if you are a person concerned with the economic and social problems of your own country even on political and patriotic grounds, and of all peoples in the world -- do what you think, do what your intelligence and your conscience suggest regarding the problems that high fertility could cause in your environment -- whether or not you still consider valid the commandment not to kill. But consider also all the paradoxes that derive from historical experience, from different human experience, from these considerations on population problems. And question also the reason for the presence of man on this earth. On religious terms there is the end of the world, and man has always had an aspiration to a world without end. Simply on biological terms, we have experience of numerous biological species that evolved and disappeared from the face of the earth. There is more than a possibility in scientific terms that the species of homo sapiens sapiens disappears also; or that many populations disappear leaving space for other populations to live on.

U. S. HISTORY FROM A "FERTILITY", AND "IMMIGRATION", POINT OF VIEW

Welcome 300 million

Let us have a look at the history of the USA from this very particular point of view: from the fertility rates of the population, the growth of the nation, and from the evolution of the moral and religious sense which was very strong at the beginning and sometimes irrational (witches, intolerance, etc.), and has been slowly diminishing in the last 50 years.

Soon after American independence at the end of the 18th century, Benjamin Franklin, on his mission to England declared himself proud of the progress his country had achieved: the USA had democratic institutions, there was scientific and technological progress, the economy was prosperous and expanding, the population of the new nation was growing with immigration and with birth rates as high as a formidable 5.5%. This is the highest birth rate statistical datum I happened to meet in documented history. In modern statistics one must also take into consideration the death rates, of course. Thomas Malthus gave the same information a completely different interpretation. Franklin was an optimist: he had confidence in life, in the life of his people on this earth especially. Malthus was a pessimist. Notice that the neomalthusians today, those who are scared of population growth, reflect the very same position of Malthus two centuries ago when the world population was much smaller, less than one billion. In 1790 in the U. S. the population was 3,200,000. In 1801 in Britain it was 10,500,000. There is more food at the disposal of every single person today than in Malthus' times, or even only fifty years ago.

The 19th century was also a period of scientific and technological progress for the USA, of political expansion, and of high birth rates, although a little less high than in the 18th century. Life was not so easy in the west where colonists emigrated from the east. The general conditions were not comfortable, but families were sound and numerous with many children.

People had confidence in life, in life on this earth and confidence in life with a moral and religious dimension. We must not forget that somehow the two phenomena go together. You do not bear many children when your material conditions are already good, but when you have confidence in life. Together with the banks, the military forts and the schools, the colonists also brought with them the churches, which were of great social meaning. Today, California seems to be the most prosperous state in the U.S., the most projected into the future. Notice a parallel which seems to be trivial but it is not: in California the population has been growing more than in the other states. In 1995 the population was 29,800,000 inhabitants. In 2005 it was 36,600,000.

The growth of the US as a nation has always been marked with the growth of the population, both with high fertility rates and also with immigration: fertility first, immigration after, as an induced phenomenon, an important but almost secondary phenomenon. Immigration has been in general a positive phenomenon for the US, up to the very present day. People from other parts of the world are admitted in, they fit in the context of other people, of other institutions that have already been created, they share the general values and contribute to the welfare of the country. From this particular point of view, we must consider the history of the U.S. not only from the Pilgrim Fathers and the coming of the first European settlers to the present day, but from earlier times. These first settlers were from the rising middle classes of England, of Europe: these classes were emerging against the feudal classes in Europe. The long history of evolution had started almost at the time of the Norman invasion, and earlier with the barbaric invasions. These colonists from the middle classes in the new continent organized themselves as a political community, and created civil and political institutions. Harvard University was founded very early, soon after they arrived. The immigrants that arrived from Europe at a later date were able to fit into this scheme, into these institutions, and contributed to the welfare of the country. Another important but almost secondary phenomenon that contributed to the growth of the population and of the nation was better agriculture and better medical science, and also the presence of a vast and rich territory. Today, with a different attitude towards life, medicine is used also to prevent life. The very first settlers from England were characterized by high fertility and high moral sense – in spite of their being irrational at times (witches, intolerance, etc.), - and by great confidence in life. High fertility is a sign of the vital driving force of a country, of a civilization, of a large social group of people, of a social class. Low fertility precedes decadence and death of that community. Both high and low fertility are almost laws of nature that precede progress and decadence respectively of a large social group, of a civilization, and are almost independent from the will of the single people and of the governance.

Before the Civil War the US was a developing country: I give the term *'developing country'* a very positive meaning, a country that is growing and developing but that is not yet at the highest of its power, of its presence and predominance in the world. After the Civil War the US became a world power but its predominance in the world came after World War I and reached its climax at the end of World War II, with the military victory and the making of the atom bomb. After 60 years, the US is still a superpower -- but in proportion the US is less influential in the world today than in 1945. Decadence has already started. Who are the peoples that dare challenge the supremacy of the US today? The Muslim peoples of the Middle East, the Chinese, the Indians, all peoples that have shown a high birth rate in the last 60 years, peoples that have also shown a high moral and religious attitude, despite the irrationality and fanatic attitude of the terrorists, and excessive nationalism. The US has shown a declining fertility in the very same period of time, and a slackening of their moral and religious sense. Europe fares worse. The Vietnamese who dared challenge the American power during the long period of their war showed a formidable 3% increase of their population under those conditions. Their vital driving force was strongest. The Arab challengers today also show high birth rates and very high moral sense – despite their irrationality, even more irrational than the Puritans in early US history.

I noticed this pattern of high fertility and general progress in many many other historical contexts, different from today's world. This is not to say that high birth rates directly cause progress and expansion. But I notice that those peoples that expanded politically and created science and material progress had been endowed, at an earlier stage of growth, with high birth rates. Europe can already be considered dead and exhausted. Also Russia has an alarmingly low birth rate. I also noticed that developing civilizations with high fertility tend to overcome older civilizations that are endowed with higher technology, with more advanced science. Powerful and well organized armies, with advanced technology --- are eventually defeated by armies of developing peoples who may be able to absorb their higher technology. The US is not going to be the most advanced country in the world forever, not for another thousand years – not even for another hundred years from now. Someone else will take their place in the world, I do not know with how much human suffering. Nothing is eternal in this world. The pyramids of Egypt are among the most important monuments of past splendour, but they are not eternal either.

Those people in the US who are in favour of abortion, of limiting the size of the family, in addition to the moral problem that they may face, a problem and an issue that is more serious than the issue on slavery in the 19th century, those people are working against the general interests of their own country: they are internal enemies; they contribute to social suicide. In addition, they do not understand the reasons behind the reasons of the progress of Asian peoples: Ted Turner, *Foreign Affairs* magazine, and the American media in general.

THE CRISIS OF 1929 AND THAT OF 2008 AS PARALLELS

The world economic crisis of 2008 in many ways resembles that of 1929 in the United States. With Roosevelt's presidency and the New Deal, that crisis passed in the following years. The current crisis, at least in Europe and in the West, will not be able to pass in the same way, though there should be more success in emerging counties: India, China, some Asian nations. The reason for this is not simply and essentially economic. It is of historical, evolutionary character, and existential in a broader sense; a low birth rate in western countries, the aging of the population, the loss of vitality and initiative, the lack of vital force. Emerging Asian countries will be aided by their new energy, their youthful, more aggressive population desirous of surpassing the West and conquering the world.

The economic crises may have been caused by diverse and varying factors. One of these could be corruption in high levels of politics and the social framework; tax evasion, discriminating legislation that favors the few, exaggerated cost of politics, financial thievery. A faulty ideology can also bring on economic depression and poverty – an example can be seen in socialist countries and in the Soviet Union. The depression in Germany after World War I may have been a result of the war itself, military defeat and the fatigue and exhaustion felt after the extreme pressure of the war and the hard conditions for peace. But the same crisis came to other countries, to the winning nations as well. I intend to describe my reflections on how the crisis was won out.

We are speaking here of economy, of an aspect of the vitality of a population, be it a single nation or a group of nations, a civilization; an aspect of vital importance, yet not the only one that characterizes a culture, that characterizes the history of mankind - as Karl Marx affirmed. Marx spoke of class conflict. I will keep in mind the formation of social classes, the conflict between classes and the evolution of social classes, in my reflections on the development of the economy and the development of a new phase in history. At the same time, I will underline another vital element: the birth rate and control of fertility, topics that are rarely covered nowadays, but that are necessary if we want to understand the evolution of human society and material progress in historical context, not only the economic aspect.

We know, or we imagine, that in the future plans of the New Deal of the President of the United States in the 1930s, there was the idea of participation in a world war and the sense of future political dominance in the world scene. Economic recovery would help sustain the necessary successive war effort, and the response to the war would bring scientific and technological research, for peace as well as war. If we look back at World War II with German eyes, the first images that come to mind are Auschwitz and Stalingrad. This is understandable. But we should also ask ourselves how Germany was able to successfully sustain its war effort for several years, industrially and economically. In 1933 Roosevelt was elected president of the United States and Hitler came to power in Germany. And parallel to the New Deal in the US, Germany's economy was picking up, with economic plans aiming at war, at world domination. Russia, too, with the errors and horrors that accompany a fateful ideology, was preparing a war economy. During the war, Russia received arms and war material from the US, but was also able to produce modern arms and tanks that were superior to those produced in Germany.

After World War II, Europe was in ruins. With help from the United States and their own means and will, the western European nations were able to begin an impressive economic revival. Unlike Roosevelt's New Deal and the recovery of Germany in the 1930s, which aimed at an imperialistic expansion, the Keynesian theories and the plans of the leaders who created a united Europe had no idea of conquering the world. There was simply a sense of cooperation between Europeans and an ideal of economic and social well-being after the rigors of the war, after two wars caused by those same Europeans. Europe lacked the energy to aim for greater things. There was still a young generation desirous of improvement. Now there are no young people. We are all old.

In 1929, among the many factors leading to the crisis, e.g. tax evasion, exploitation of the less privileged, etc., we can see that one of the causes of the crisis was overproduction of consumer goods, and that production was in the hands of a very few, the great industrialists, the great financiers, who also had a direct influence of governing, on the presidency. The GNP grew but the earnings were fictitious. In preceding years, the internal competitive (and often fierce, immoral and illegal) commercial wars between economic groups had brought on an enormous growth in production, but a drop in the number of groups of competitors. Karl Marx had prophesized that competition would reduce the number of the wealthy and would exasperate the proletariat. The proletariat would then be in a position to overthrow the wealthy and install a proletarian dictatorship. The crisis of 1929 seemed to be the situation predicted by Marx. And many Americans accused Roosevelt, for his political and economic choices, of being a Communist.

It has always been said that America is the land of opportunity, that anyone could realize the American dream. Social classes didn't exist; all men were equal and had equal opportunities. One of the most well-known cases was that of Abraham Lincoln: born in humble circumstances, he rose to become president of the United States, and be considered one of the greatest Americans. The almost illiterate immigrant arriving from Italy or another European country no longer found himself face to face with a feudal land baron, but was treated with less social distance. Perhaps nationalism might cause a few problems. But it is not true to say that there were no social classes in America. They were there, based on wealth and social status. Certainly less rigid than in Europe. An extreme example is the caste system in India, where the social division had a religious connotation.

The Pilgrim Fathers who settled on the east coast of the continent were not the typical poor coming from underdeveloped countries. They weren't at the bottom of the social ladder, nor were they humble peasants looking for better conditions and a better life in a new social context. They were part of the British middle classes, which were beginning to be characterized with human values, with capabilities not limited to the economic field, with a sense of initiative, with aggressiveness, with religious ideals sometimes bordering on fanaticism. As has happened more recently with modern ideologies – almost artificial religions, and fundamentalism in third world countries. The evolution of European societies, the British society in this case, had begun long before. The middle class in Great Britain was gaining ground in relation to the old feudal nobility; with religious ideals and moral energy, with difficulties and struggles to affirm its identity.

These representatives of the middle classes built a new nation on a new continent, following their ideals, which were not strictly economic. We must keep in mind the religious motivation. Coming from Europe, these representatives were the most active, the most intelligent, and the ones with most hope for the future. They built a prosperous nation, and those who came later were able to fit in and contribute to the economic well-being of the new country which was already in a state of vigorous development. Some had more luck than others, and distinguished themselves. Later they tended to feel morally and socially superior to those who weren't as able or as fortunate, and who then made up a lower social class.

In this early period, the birth rate was very high, and continued so through the 19th century and for part of the 20th. Only in the past decades has it begun to decline. With a loss of vital energy, of ideals, of religious and moral commitment, and with diminishing political prestige in the world. We must remember how the native cultures were treated and the African peoples enslaved.

When the crisis suddenly hit in 1929, a crisis caused by over-production and by the immoral concentration of wealth in the hands of a very few, the actions of the new president aimed at looking ahead. To put the nation back on its feet, on a new base, with different actors. The *common man*, the almost-proletariat that Marx described, became the central figure in the new historical period, not only economic. He was the true motor. The US president tended to favor the lower classes, against the upper classes, against the trusts, against great industrialists. Something similar had happened in Tudor England, under Elizabeth I, who tended to favor the emerging middle classes against the feudal lords. Middle classes that were productive and active, against nobles who impeded the monarchy. At length these would reveal themselves to have been a factor in the development of modern democracy. Roosevelt used the *common man* as opposed to the great industrialists. All Americans regarded him as a father-figure. They wrote to him, and he answered through his secretaries. The new means of mass communication gave him popularity. Americans felt that they were democratic, or at least more democratic than in the past. Actually the presidency as a political office was reinforced, and the president had more power than before. More power than when he was influenced by the big trusts. Not that this was necessarily negative. But in the long run, the consequences could be serious.

It won't be necessary to describe here all the plans and actions of the New Deal, from devaluation of the dollar to facilitate recovery, to the great public works and to the Manhattan Project and scientific research. But it is useful to remember that all Americans were offered the opportunity to participate actively in economic recovery, yet recovery was not only economic. Not all Americans were able to profit from the opportunities offered by the president. Not all Americans were active or positive. Who? Why? At this point we face moral or social questions, or even questions regarding luck. New intermediate middle classes developed, on various levels, less distinct than in the past and in feudal times. The most active people emerged, the *common man*, the typical average American, patriotic, technically skilled, eager, and full of faith in his future and the future of his nation. The great works of the president, and lesser-known projects of capable men, moved the country forward, in a great leap for the American economy and a great leap for the history of mankind. But the New Deal was not eternal. The vitality of America, of the *common man* couldn't last forever. The *common man* acquired wealth and moved up the social ladder, and tended to hold on to his status as long as possible, just as the USA tends to maintain its position of superpower in the world today. Even the class of the *common man* tends to fossilize.

The crisis of 1929 was local, American, but even then the consequences were felt all over the world. There was already a certain degree of globalization. It's a natural factor that can be resisted – or favored - only up to a certain point. In the end, however, globalization cannot be resisted, since all populations can communicate. Even in the past, remote or recent. In the United States of the 1960s there was a car for every three Americans, while in Europe the ratio was much lower, even if there was recovery from the war. Today in my region of Italy, there are seventy-five cars for every hundred inhabitants, everybody has a mobile phone, and food isn't lacking. What more do we want? Is there still room for expansion and economic growth? Do we have any ideals other than reaching and maintaining a level of economic well-being and certain social services? Very few children are born in our society. We fear the future, economic as well. Asian countries are imitating and copying all that we are doing in the west. They want the same number of cars, and they can build them. The desire to imitate and to go beyond the west is foremost, but the ability to imitate and to go beyond the west are decisive factors. They can manufacture their own weapons, even the atomic bomb. Other world populations don't seem to have absorbed western scientific thought and technology as yet, and so are still not in a position to pass the west. China, India, and other Asian countries are. With some motives that are not strictly economic. Like during the years of the New Deal, not all Americans were able to improve their status, to take advantage of the opportunities offered by the president.

In my region, a certain degree of recovery was evident after World War II. People wanted to improve their economic status, and the USA and more advanced European countries were seen as models. Emigration was strong. Young people went to school, and the schools were of good quality. Townships organized night schools. Young people worked during the day and learned the rudiments of technical design and of economics in the evenings. Returning ex-emigrants brought back experience, technical knowledge, a force of initiative that is at the base of any economic or social recovery. The expression *metalmezzadri* (sharecroppers who worked as metalworkers in industry) was coined. These were the farmers who worked forty hours in the factories around Pordenone, as unskilled laborers at first, and who also worked in the fields in the old sharecropping system. They wanted to improve their lot. They worked, they learned, and the most active set up their own businesses. All the North-east was characterized by this small industry. Without help from the central government in Rome. The only time Rome came to the aid of the Friuli Venezia Giulia region was after the earthquake of 1976. At that time national and international aid was magnificent, and moving. The north-east was in the midst of a booming economy, and help from the government and from foreign sources was an additional element in this economic growth. Rather like a miniature

Marshall Plan. The funds weren't wasted, as in other Italian regions or in other areas of the world. First the factories and the infrastructures were rebuilt, as a springboard for the economy. Friuli, and the north-east, once among the poorest regions in northern Italy, became one of the richest regions in Europe. But again, we note that development never goes on infinitely.

Would the central government or the international community respond in the same way if a new cataclysm hit Friuli? And would the result be the same? After the opening of the European Union to other countries after the fall of the Soviet Union in 1989, with all the financial aid that has gone to these countries, especially to East Germany, success isn't as evident or as dramatic as the reconstruction of Europe after World War II. Europe has aged, all Europe, eastern and western.

It was these *metalmezzadri*, these returning emigrants, who started up new businesses. It was the night school students, after a heavy day of work. It was the students coming out of technical schools with good skills. It was the people from earlier generations who had suffered as emigrants and throughout two world wars. Their healthy and numerous families had a strong moral base, religious in character (sometimes not very rational). These were the people who brought the progress we enjoy now, not the young people of today, even if they know how to use computers and cellphones better than we – the older "fossils" – do. Today it's Chinese youth, in factories where they work long hours and sleep at their workplace, unprotected by Union laws – they are the ones who are building a future for their people. Here in Italy, the central government had organized good schools, beginning before the war, and young people were eager to learn and to improve their lot. We can remember the fortunate international situation that enabled western European countries to build a new world, a prosperous economy. In Poland, for example, people weren't very different from Italians from north-east Italy, but historical circumstances and ideology didn't allow the Poles to build a prosperous economy like ours.

In the case of north-east Italy, of western Europe, of Roosevelt's New Deal, along with appropriate political leadership there were many people eager and able to improve their lives. There were many young people, unlike today.

Now there are many old people and few young. Not everyone knew how to take advantage of the opportunities that the president and the government offered. They remained at the tail end of progress, of the evolution of a people that had begun long before. First the feudal class in Europe, then the middle classes, with intermediate levels, then the *common man*, representative of the low middle class, and then those who remained in the lower classes.

As for developing countries in other areas of the world, some are moving ahead, some not, and some slowly. Those that are developing are usually countries with a history of old civilization, which have already contributed to the creation of science and technology. Young people from these countries usually have a talent for mathematics and abstract thinking. Students coming to schools in the USA from India, China and the Middle East usually excel in technical and economic studies. An Indian student of nineteen arriving in the USA with a green card for studies in economics, or physics, and whose IQ is similar to that of his American peer, will receive higher marks for a variety of reasons. In his school in India he will have studied other subjects such as history and philosophy, while the American is more ignorant. The young Indian will know other languages, and will have a superior moral fiber; he will want to emerge but also to repay his parents for their sacrifices. The environment he comes from is characterized by a superior moral and idealistic tone, which westerners regard as irrational, medieval. All this gives him an advantage.

In our world we complain about unfair competition when the Chinese and Indians copy our patents, we complain that those who work in Italy pay fewer taxes, that a Chinese laborer works many more hours and is treated badly, not according to our Union laws. This perhaps is true. When you're fighting for existence, this happens. But we reason with our minds, following our convictions and the moral standard that we have built up over time. It wasn't always like this. Not so long ago our *metalmezzadri* worked just like the Chinese, and it was their work that brought us to this situation. Our young people once worked hard to be able to study and learn. The Chinese now work long hours, but they also want to learn, and, what is more important, they are able to learn. Not everyone is. They have values and skills. Many others, near to us and further away, don't have the ability to learn.

India is a developing country: its society is made up of castes. These were legally abolished with independence in 1947, but in reality they still hold sway, with effects that are surprising and sometimes dramatic for westerners. Indians say that the castes cannot be compared with social classes in Europe, even those in the darkest period of medieval times. I don't agree. They are indeed particular; supposedly society was thus organized to satisfy the desires of a god. Christian missionaries who come to India to set up schools for the *Dalit*, the untouchables, disturb the social balance created by God. A *Dalit* who can read and write, and who has skills, is no longer an untouchable. Even in Europe kings were once kings by the grace of God, and the Pope crowned the Emperor. Then, as society evolved, with new philosophical concepts and with modernity, kings became kings by the grace of God and the will of the nation. More a formula than a real concept.

Castes were formed with Brahmanism, with the religion that the Hindus brought with the arrival of the Aryans in the 2nd millenium B.C. and which later developed. At first it had racial connotations, even of color. India is an immense country that cannot be compared with Italy, England or other individual western countries, but with Europe, with the entire West. A civilization parallel with ours, with surprising similarities and points of contact. As Indian civilization we should include Pakistan, Bangladesh, Sri Lanka, part of Afghanistan and Indonesia. Islam brought significant changes to the structures of society in these great civilizations. India is now a country in a period of enormous and rapid growth. Economically speaking, today many people distinguish themselves beyond their original social group: great merchants, industrialists, some scientists. Naturally they must have a certain level of instruction, but they come to make up a new social class, independent of caste.

This new emerging class has become a leader in the economic growth of modern India, but it is not destined to remain forever. India now has a GNP that equals that of the largest western countries, but those who produce this wealth are a minority of the population, perhaps around 150 million people, who represent the new emerging classes. A great part of the population remains in conditions of extreme poverty and cultural backwardness. But there is still a margin for growth in the future. The evolution of society into these new classes has just begun. If the world economy is interconnected and globalized, if technical information still comes from the West, India has taken giant strides.

The emerging social classes are not only characterized by industrialists and merchants; there are also those made up of people who are inspired by magnanimous ideals, even irrational ones. They are the new social classes, they create something new. They have political aims for their community. The religious and moral sense is reinforced, at times with a touch of fanaticism, like suicide terrorists, who die for an ideal which is difficult for us to comprehend. We see the "Arab springs" and the sense of people fighting the status quo of their political regimes, and against the West. Economic growth is only one aspect of the global development of these peoples. Even the Pilgrim Fathers who emigrated from England to build a new place for themselves on the new continent were animated by ideals and a certain aggressiveness that reminds us of these peoples who are emerging.

Here in the West, our ideals are now limited. We want a prosperous economy; we want free social services, and a democracy which we erroneously consider a supreme good. To be elected, politicians have to make promises that they cannot maintain. Public debt is growing. Those who work and produce are treated like well-intentioned slaves – like the small businessmen of the north-east. Dishonesty in politics is an open secret, but political dishonesty and corruption are rampant in other continents, even in developing countries. Dishonesty and corruption are a factor in the current decadence in the economic field, but they are not the only reason for the lack of vitality and impulse. A wrong ideal, a mistaken ideology; these definitely contribute to a decrease in economic growth. A centralized socialist economy brought Russia and eastern Europe to economic disaster. The application of similar theories in the western world today – excessive taxation with resulting suffocation of production – is leading to the road to ruin. Institutional honesty, political honesty of those in government, but even the honesty of normal citizens – a civic sense of duty as seems to exist in northern European countries – could all help alleviate this situation, these prospects. But the basic problem remains. Where is our energy for the future, to improve our lot on this earth? We're old. There aren't enough young people, not enough children. There is no future. We have no trust in our future. Other populations have that kind of trust. And it looks like they are aggressively and violently eager to overtake the West.

Summary:

The crisis of 1929, like that of 2008, was caused primarily by overproduction of consumer goods that had no outlet on the market. It might be said that another cause came from man himself: excessive greed, exploitation and poor treatment of those who produced the goods, and legislation made to favor excessively those already in a position of prestige. All this has a value of social class. The crisis in Europe after World War I, for both winners and losers, was a crisis of fatigue after the strain of war, particularly in the production of goods. Here, too, the crisis had a connotation of class. The classes that gained wealth, that were socially and politically strengthened, in the long run tend to solidify and to become less creative; they simply want to continue enjoying the wealth and their privileges.

The recovery from the crisis, in America and Germany after 1933, in other western European countries after World War II, also has a connotation of social class. The president of the United States used the leverage of the *common man*, who belonged to a low, but not the lowest, class. A man of values, with some technical skills, desirous of improving his life, patriotic and attached to the land. The president promoted great public works, scientific research on a grand scale, devalued the dollar to favor all those who wanted to create or continue in business – this definitely has a connotation of class. He favored the *common man* against the class of great economic power that had dominated the political and economic scene up to then. This powerful class was made up of the men who had contributed to the great leap forward that produced wealth, but that also led to the crisis. Their class was fossilizing. They accused the US president of being a communist. In the recovery, in the great plans of the president, the economy is only one aspect that we analyze. Actually, among the greater and recondite ideals of the president, there was also the ideal of world political predominance; there was also World War II. As it was for Hitler's Germany. And for the

Russia of Stalin, who managed to produce a great number of tanks, but not as many consumer goods – thanks to an excess of obsessive economic ideology that will lead to the final fall.

The political and economic theories of Adam Smith, *laissez-faire* and non-intervention of the state in the economy; the theories of J.M. Keynes of guided and intelligent intervention of government in the economy; or even in part the theories of socialism, of good socialism on earth, can still be valid and effective – but they are not an absolute. They are not laws of nature like the laws of physics. They can be effective in certain social environments when the people have reached a certain level of maturity. But they are not valid forever.

After World War II Europe's economies recovered along the lines traced by J.M. Keynes. But Europe was exhausted, and didn't have enough energy for a great leap forward, Europeans aimed only at reconstruction and the enjoyment of a good economy under the protection of a foreign power: the USA on the one hand, the Soviet Union on the other. The crisis of 2008 resembles the crisis of 1929 but cannot really be compared in the same way, at least in Europe. The crisis may seem less dramatic than in 1929, because the modern world has provided some cushioning through social security. But there cannot be recovery because we cannot trust in the *common man*, the man of skills and strong will coming from the lower classes; we cannot trust in young people. The low birth rate and the aging of the population are not only a social cost, but they also weaken society, rendering it incapable of improvement, and bringing it to the brink of disaster, to its disappearance from the face of the earth. Asian economies are prospering. Even in the face of a world crisis linked to globalization, India still has a margin for growth. New social classes, outside the caste system, have been born. Classes that are dynamic. They still haven't reached the final stages of the *common man*. In the evolution of their societies there's space for development and growth, not only economic. The Asian nations want to dominate the world, not only economically. They hate, and aim to rule the West.

VICO IN BRIEF

His principal work is _La Scienza Nuova_ (The New Science): three editions, the first in 1725, the last in 1744. The title refers to science. The science of Man, the rational study of Man, of his existence, his evolution, what he has done, his history. In schools he should be studied not only as a man of letters, a philosopher, but also as a man of science. He is the creator of a new science. Vico speaks about the evolution of man. Who before him? Psychological evolution, of the mind first of all. Its famous _"degnità"_ (axiom/authoritative maxim): _Men first feel without comprehension, then they feel with a perturbed and moved soul, and lastly they reflect with a pure mind."_ Which is not insignificant.

Vico has insights, vigorous allusions to even the physical evolution of man. He speaks about human beasts that evolve, and become men. Normal men, rational, as modern man is. He speaks of the giants of the Bible and Greek mythology. They would be traces in human memory of men from earlier eras. Traces from the infancy of mankind, flashes of collective dreams – like a man who in his maturity remembers moments from his early childhood, in his Freudian unconscious. A collective unconscious. He speaks of Gauls and Germans, giant-like in stature, endowed with fury in battle, but little power of reason, against the more rational Romans, as written by Caesar and Tacitus. Who before him had expressed a similar concept of evolution? An intuition that preceded by a century the theories of evolution of Charles Darwin. And Freud.

We cannot speak of an influence of Vico on Darwin. But a juxtaposition of Darwin to Vico has been made over the years by numerous modern scholars since the publication of On the Origin of Species, beginning with Bertrando Spaventa.

Vico has been cited as a forerunner of various 18th and 19th-century philosophies. Hegel for one. Vico's pedagogy is in line with J.J.Rousseau, though it's clearer and more defined than Rousseau's. For Vico, sentiment has maximum value in the face of the Reason of the Enlightenment. Reason, however, is a vital component of human life. Wolf's Homeric question is practically an extension of that of Vico. To Isaiah Berlin, Herder seems identical to Vico, though a real link has not been shown, nor an influence, even indirect, on Vico's part.

Benedetto Croce affirmed that during a visit to Venice, Montesquieu purchased a copy of the first edition of La Scienza Nuova, and that the volume was part of his library in his castle. Indirectly, Vico might have had a slight influence on him, on his spirit of laws that evolve in time. Then there is the concept that man creates religion, poetry, the arts, the sciences, civil institutions, and all material things. Man creates religion – before Feuerbach. And yet Vico remains a practising Catholic, believing in the death and resurrection of Jesus Christ. A contradiction, even if a secondary one, according to Croce. A man of great intellect who remains a man of the people, maintaining certain incredible infantile beliefs in the face of the spelled-out reasoning of modern times.

All great men show their greatness in one aspect their lives, while revealing *naiveté* and weaknesses in other areas of their private lives. Perhaps in Vico's case it was an attempt to mask certain new philosophical ideas from the inquisitional authorities of his time. And yet, no. Vico's philosophy and science could not be understood in his time, including the concept that man created religions. This stands without contradiction. But certain ideas about religion couldn't be understood before the *Second Vatican Council*. It's as though a modern scientist, astronomer or nuclear physicist, possessed knowledge of the world and physics and still believed in the death and resurrection of Jesus Christ. And down with all those scientists who self-proclaim themselves as atheists, and aware or not, consider science their own particular divinity, their absolute. A divinity created by man, a divinity that consists in ideas, ideology, not raw material such as gold or clay or the marble of heathen idols.

Vico is universal. Indians say that Hegel was a racist, one who ignored their contributions to humanity's progress: their mathematics and their science above all. Hegel is the primary source of many current ideologies. From Greek and Indian philosophies come religious movements, ideologies that have even created misunderstanding in Christianity; for example Buddhism in India, Platonism in the west.

Vico, with his grandiose intuitions, well-balanced in the context of Humanism, is the pure scientist. He studies the concrete fact, man and his evolution through history, and remains a believer in Jesus Christ. In the 18th century his interest in science is remarkable; we recognize it in his *Autobiography*, even if his main interests are poetry, philosophy and law.

Vico didn't have the luck that others had. He doesn't write well. His ideas are far ahead of his time; he jumps ahead of the philosophy of the Enlightnement before the Enlightenment has even made itself clear. He goes back over his thoughts and corrects them, all distractions that impede comprehension of his insights. A vision of the world that along general lines is essentially simple and rational, like Darwin's theory of the evolution of the species.

René Descartes explained his scientific method, his theory of knowledge: When you have a problem, analyze it carefully from all points of view, from all contradictions that may arise. This leads you to true knowledge. The foundation of knowledge and science. No, says Vico. This is *"certum"*, that is partial knowledge. You have *"verum"*, *"true knowledge"*, that is knowledge *"per causas"*, when you make it yourself. God can know the world, nature, because he made it. Man can know his history, because he has made it.

But don't read Vico's works if you don't have specialistic intentions. He doesn't write well, as did Machiavelli, J.J. Rousseau, and others who were more fortunate. Nowadays he's seen as a Catholic. Predominant ideologies suggest leaving him in the background for this reason. In fact, his science could be accepted both as the work and intuition of a believer and of a non-believer. Simply a scientific work, a study of nature, of human nature in this case.

All German philosophy of the 19th and 20th centuries seems to be in perfect harmony with Vico. More extensive and more complete, it's understandable, but not better balanced. We can find an illustrious precedent in the Arab, Ibn Khaldun (Tunis 1332 - 1406 Cairo). Vico didn't know of Ibn Khaldun, a man of a different culture, who was famous throughout the Arab world but unknown in the west. The Arabs compare Ibn Khaldun to Machiavelli, and consider Ibn Khaldun superior. In addition to offering political advice to governing bodies, to his prince, Ibn Khaldun offered an interpretation of history, describing the evolution of Berbers from a primitive stage to one much more rational and civilized, and then to final decadence. He underlined the value of education of feeling, and the importance of a religious sense in the evolution of civilizations. Religious and moral sense as a value in itself, and as an element of development in all the Berber tribes. And he also underlined the value and the implications of demographic growth.

DARWIN AND VICO

Charles Darwin's (1809-1882) theory of the evolution of the species is a novelty in the fields of life and culture of western civilization, and of all civilizations that have followed on this earth. This is by no means a simple Copernican revolution in which the terms are overturned, nor is it a synthetic opinion by which a thesis and an antithesis conclude in a synthesis. It is something that man had never thought about before, something he had never noticed before in his exploration of the world and of nature. Hence, all living creatures including human beings adapt to their environment, they fight for their survival, evolve physically during a long period of time first, then their behaviour evolves while their nervous system and brain become more and more complex. It's not important if today we find limits in the formulation of Darwin's theories: on the whole, the theory of the evolution of the species is absolutely valid scientifically speaking. However, the initial questions—What is life? / Who created life?—still do not find an adequate reply.

Before Charles Darwin another man of science who was not well known, the Neapolitan G.B. Vico (1668-1744), realizes through intuition that there are laws regarding the evolution of humans: above all their mental evolution which is both intellectual and affective, but also their physical evolution or evolution of the human body. Vico is considered a philosopher and a man of letters, yet he is absolutely a scientist as well. His "Scienza Nuova" or "New Science" is his most important work, dealing with the science of man, in the sense of man as the creator of his world and his history. During the course of time man evolves according to the pattern of the three ages: the age of the gods, the age of heroes and the age of rational men or age of reason. At first man creates religions, myths, poetry, while during the course of time he becomes a more rational being creating philosophy, mathematics and sciences before his decadence, whereby he returns to a phase of barbarity. This, although extremely synthesized, is Vico's concept of evolution through phases.

Together with this intellectual and psychological evolution per phases, which is rather energetic, regarding his attitude and ability to understand the world around him, Vico also seems to notice a physical evolution of man, an evolution of his physical body during lengthy periods of man's history. First of all, he finds traces in the narratives contained in ancient documents of the history of man, which were available to him during his lifetime. In the books of the Bible, before the universal deluge, men had become giants: they rebelled against God and had become evil. In Greek mythology, giants who are driven to hell are also mentioned. In the "Odyssey" we find the most famous of all giants: Polyphemus. These were men who had strong limbs, capable of violent passions but not endowed with reason, another example being the biblical Goliath who was killed by David. These could be considered traces, deformed memories of a former humanity of which we have little or no recollection, of a humanity which has grown and evolved, traces of memories that modern man is trying to rebuild at an individual level, in some kind of Freudian unconscious.

As far as ancient times are concerned, Vico is conditioned by the culture of his time which believed that the creation of the world went only as far back as six thousand years, as would appear from a rather superficial reading of the Bible. However, Vico does use expressions that render this era infinitely far back in time, for example when human beasts with extremely robust senses, fervid imagination and lack of reason wandered in the forests. He uses expressions such as "and if, on the other hand, we counted the years as the Chinese do". Vico has a clear feeling that the periods of history go much further back than six thousand years, as was believed in his time.

What is also interesting is Vico's observation regarding the Germans and the Gauls, those barbaric populations of whom Caesar and Tacitus speak of in ancient times, considered no longer mythic and dealt with using more precise information. This information is taken from the outside, from the Romans, from a civilization that found itself in another level of evolution, not from the same Germans or their myths. The German barbarians are tall, capable of a tremendous fury in war when faced with the Romans, who were shorter in stature, but more rational: as if two civilizations at different levels of their evolution met and clashed. After a long period of time the German and Gallic barbarians were also to evolve intellectually, psychologically and physically, and were to become rational men in modern times. Already by the first half of the 18th century, Vico was questioning himself on how the most primitive populations of other continents were intellectually and physically, promising himself to gather information from missionaries who had been to the lands of Patagonia.

Vico's intuitions seemed imprecise, as were imprecise and insufficient the information that were available to him in his time and in his environment. A century later Hegel and the German philosophers could have more complete information at their disposal. Most of his information comes from his direct knowledge of the ancient classical world and from the Bible. From this information, together with the rational mentality of his time, Vico creates a new science, the science of man, the evolution of man. A contemporary of his, Anton Lazzaro Moro (1687-1764), also a scientist but in another branch of human knowledge, is interested in the fossils that he finds in the mountains and in the effects of volcanic eruptions. From his personal observation of nature, and from information on the eruption on the island of Santorini in Greece which took place in a historical and classical epoch, much in the same way as Vico, Moro formulated his theory which is the basis of modern geology.

We cannot state that Vico had anticipated Darwin, nor that he actually had a certain influence in the formulation of his theories on the evolution of the species. However, we must note that both are creators of a new science: the evolution of man. Both are on the same wavelength and deserve to be considered on the same level. It is unimportant whether or not archaeology has yet to demonstrate the existence of human beings with disproportioned limbs, as held by Vico. It is unimportant whether or not we notice many imprecisions in Vico, and whether or not his way of writing is as clear or linear as it should be for such a level of scientific research. This contributed to his being isolated, his not becoming well known and his being neglected for a long time. His intuitions represented a novelty and were original for his time, even if the tradition of neoplatonism, of Humanism to which Vico belonged (Pico, Ficino, Manetti, etc.) may have given him some clues. However, the structure of his whole system of thought is very clear, grandiose, balanced and relatively easy to understand.

His whole system could be considered a model of materialism, yet it could also be accepted as he really intended: the hand of God and Providence that guides the history of man, with God as the creator of the universe, and with man who participates in some way in His creation. Man who evolves physically and mentally, and creates religions, poetry, language, arts, mathematics, science, civil institutions, material things and all of history itself. Philosopher Bertrando Spaventa noticed this relationship Vico – Darwin back in 1875, comparing natural sciences and human sciences. And in the wake of positivist thinking of his time, he considered this evolution of man on pure scientific and materialistic terms – without any Divine Providence or intervention of God from the outside.

IBN KHALDUN AND VICO

Arab historian Ibn Khaldun (Tunis 1332, Cairo 1406) is the first scholar to deal with history from an evolutionary point of view, before Vico formulated his theory of the *courses and recourses* of civilizations, of the evolution of institutions, and of the fantasy and creativity of man. Without going so far as to say that man creates religions arts and sciences, in his *Muqaddimah*, (*An Introduction to History*) he clearly notices our patterns of the growth of civilizations, including the growth of the population.

As some kind of social organization is formed, civilization results (*'umran*). The Arabic word, derived from a root which means *'to build up, to develop'*, is also used by Ibn Khaldun in the further sense of *'population'*. When a social organization grows more populous, a larger and better *'umran* results. This growth in numbers, with a corresponding growth in civilization, finally culminates in the higher form of sedentary culture man is able to achieve. He is mainly interested in the factor he calls *'asabiyah*, that is *solidarity*, *group feeling, group consciousness*, and in *religion* as a unifying factor for all the peoples of a geographical area. He analyzes Islam's role in cementing state power, in building and preserving larger and more stable empires. In the views of Ibn Khaldun dynasties arise from successfully marshalling this *group feeling* which he believed originated from respect of blood ties or something akin to that. Because of the difficult conditions the Bedouins were exposed to in the desert, he saw the Bedouins as most capable of developing and harnessing *group feeling*. He also noted the fearless manner in which they fought and subdued others – seeing in their *savagery*, the seeds of royal power. However, he also saw the Bedouins as wild and anarchic – as all too capable of plundering the possessions of others, and destroying the civilizations of those whom they conquered, citing specifically the ruination of the civilizations of Yemen, Syria, Iraq, and the Sudan after Bedouin conquests. He thus argued that for the Bedouins to develop royal leadership, they needed the strong influence of a religion such as Islam, which he saw as crucial to the initial success of the Arabs. It was the cohesive force of Islam that enabled the Arabs to combine strong *group feelings* with the political leadership that was necessary to win and sustain stable royal dynasties. He attributed their subsequent decline to their neglect of religion, and of loosing their *group feeling* and leadership skills in the course of acquiring wealth and urban comforts. Interestingly enough, also for Ibn Khaldun growth and morals go somewhat together, as linked parallel phenomena.

In developing these elaborate theories on the rise and fall of dynasties, he suggests that a nation that is defeated and comes under the rule of another quickly perishes, citing the case of Persia after its Arab conquest. He also repeatedly emphasizes the widely held belief that *the common people follow the religion of the ruler* – the same concept of *cuius regio eius religio* in Europe after the peace of Augusta in the 16th century. What is implicit in his writings, Indian scholars contend, is that Islam, rather than being a revolutionary egalitarian force as often claimed, was more the instrument for developing tribal leadership, and the means of cementing political control over those who shared in the *group feelings* of the ruling clans, or by extension, a means of controlling those that did not necessarily share in the *group feelings* of the ruling élites.

Although Ibn Khaldun clearly attributes the later decline of the Arabs to the neglect of religion and to the wealth and comfort of urban life, he does not consider it as the end of a historical cycle as Vico would have, the final phase. This was also the case of Persia and of other countries that were conquered militarily by the Arabs just when they were losing their *vital driving force* at the end of their vital cycles – whereas the Arabs were at the very beginning of their cycle, - when they were still *barbarians*. Ibn Khaldum himself reports a story that the very name Berber derives from *barbarah,* a nickname given to them by an ancient king of Yemen who fought against them, when he heard their barbarian way of speaking.

Ibn Khaldun seems to be a devout Muslim and a believer in spite of his honest and rational thinking. More or less the same way Vico was a devout catholic with the faith of a simple man - in spite of his daring philosophical conclusion that religion is a creation of man. However, Ibn Khaldun considers religion more than Vico does as a Machiavellian means in the hands of the rulers in order to rule – a bit like Marx in the 19th century. Perhaps this is the reason why Islamic scholars like to compare

Ibn Khaldun to Machiavelli, not to Vico, and consider him superior to Machiavelli because he neglects religion and does only consider the political and military aspect of a civilization. Machiavelli lived one century after Ibn Khaldun, they stress, but they fail to notice the fact that they lived in two different civilizations. For Vico religion is also a value per se - as is poetry. And both Vico and Ibn Khaldun seem to be sincere believers in their God.

Although Ibn Khaldun's writings stress the role of Islam in the Arab success, it is not possible to conclude from his writings (as some Islamist scholars have attempted) a claim to the universality and superiority of Islam, and speak of its *natural tendency* towards raising the cultural levels of societies that adopted the faith. That Islam was more a political tool (than an inherently more advanced scientific, philosophical or cultural system) is borne out by how the Umayyads sought cultural inspiration from the very civilizations they had sought to supplant and replace. This was even more the case with the Abbasids who succeeded the Umayyads. Both invited scholars (and those brought as slaves), encouraged or coerced them to translate scientific and philosophical texts from a variety of ancient and contemporary sources including Greek, Syriac, Babylonian and Indian. Some of these texts were subsequently translated into Latin in Spain and found their way to influencing medieval Europe and all modern western civilization. Another peculiar case of **transculturation**. Transculturation is different from the modern day notion of Multiculturalism in western countries. The Indians today are especially resentful on this point against the Arabs and Islam in general for their conquest and Islamization of Sind, and for their pretension of cultural and religious superiority on India.

In narrating events and situations Ibn Khaldun clearly notices the pattern of high birth rates in populations that are evolving, although he does not stress on it – the same way modern scholars do when writing history text books for the schools. He also notes the evolution of the moral attitude. In his philosophy of history Vico does draw our attention to the evolution of customs and of the moral attitude of people in various phases of evolution, but never mentions numerical growth or shrinking of populations. This is a liberty I am taking, a fact that I notice in the evolution of various civilizations.

G.B. VICO

Gian Battista Vico (1668-1744) is one of the greatest figures of Western thought of all times. His name is relatively little known even in texts of philosophy, history and cultural matters in general: this is essentially due to the novelty of his thought, and to the fact that he was unable to express himself efficiently in his writings. He is a humble man with little talent that cannot express the volcanic genius of his intuitions. His thought is so advanced with respect to the culture of his time yet his ideas are expressed in such a non-linear and unclear way, that it is understandable for the modern reader how he was neglected in his day because of the rigour of eighteenth century Enlightenment mentality. We can better understand his philosophic thought, in the light of all the philosophy of Idealism that he had anticipated. He went beyond the philosophy of Idealism in that his concept of Divine Providence which is overlooking the history of men - can be considered as he really intended it as a believer, as a Christian believer, though a simple one as Croce said. A Divine Providence the philosophers of Idealism considered a form of Hegelian *"Idea"*. Moreover, Vico lived in early eighteenth century Naples, not in France or in England which were the centres of both European Enlightenment and Western civilisation at the time; or in Germany that was becoming the new centre of Western culture in the romantic epoch – the latter along the same lines that Vico had already anticipated. Had Vico lived two centuries earlier, when the Italian Renaissance was at the centre of European culture, his fame and fortune could have been different. There are a few centres for Vico Studies in Italy and in America today, and he is going to be known also in Asia.

It is only natural that every civilisation celebrates its own heroes, its own great men: the men of their homeland rather than those of other civilisations. This tendency was particularly evident in the nineteenth and twentieth centuries, in a climate which was at first romantic and then nationalistic, with evident instrumental intentions on the part of the politicians in office. The Germans stated that German philosophy was superior to French philosophy; German music superior to Italian music; that their science and technology were superior and that they themselves were superior. This superior German mentality continued until the end of the Second World War when defeat led to soul-searching and self examination: "If our greatest historical figures were superior how could they have led us through two disastrous wars?" In this climate of nationalistic culture the presence of a humble southern man was a nuisance: a Neapolitan who brilliantly anticipates all the philosophy of German Idealism is better ignored. In this climate of modern Western civilisation we notice, en passant, how the philosophical ideas of southern Italians – not only Vico but also Telesio, Bruno, Campanella and, more recently, Croce and Gentile – are so similar to the philosophical thoughts of northern Germans, more so than to that of the French or English. Sicily and Southern Italy, in general, are considered Western civilisations to the same degree as Immanuel's Kant eastern Prussia.

Vico does not know how to write; he does not know how to express himself with good style. Inside one of Vico's thoughts another is born, and so Vico modifies and retouches his thought, sometimes making blunders and by using mistaken information or argumentation. I would not advise the reading of _La Scienza Nuova_ or his other minor works to those who are not specialists in the field. However, his global thought is clear, and relatively simple. His concept of knowledge, his whole philosophical system is pure materialism (yet more serene than Hegel) in which there is room for divinity and Christian transcendence: much in the same way that the modern scientist who dedicates his studies to material things such as the world of nature – can believe in God the Almighty. Man himself is the creator of his world: he participates in divine creation and thus can understand what he himself creates: his history.

Vico states that man creates religions (and poetry) in a certain moment during the evolution of his civilisation a century before Ludwig Feuerbach (1804-1872) does, yet with more valuable arguments. Vico deals with social classes, their evolution and the struggles between these classes long before Karl Marx (1818-1883) does. Marx knows and appreciates the philosophy of Vico. On reading the _Manifesto_ I had the impression that this pamphlet was written just after having read about the patricians and plebeians in the *Scienza Nuova,* with the difference that Vico's intention is simply that of better knowing the world of mankind as it is; Marx, on the other hand, wants to change it.

The idea of continuous evolution, and the fact that in a certain moment in his evolution man is more rational with respect to a more primitive moment - is a clear concept for Vico. Marx, instead, wants to block history and evolution arbitrarily, and install a proletarian dictatorship, with no aspiration towards a transcendental dimension. Religion for Marx is, in fact, an instrument in the hands of the governing class, to subdue the lower or the proletariat: which to the modern man could be considered true and realistic in some historical frameworks; religion is not even considered as a creation or as a primordial need of mankind, as is poetry. It seems as though Marx has not understood this omnicomprehensive aspect of man in the sense of society, the total or complete man according to the more serene vision of the Humanist and Renaissance epochs.

To Vico evolution is not solely of psychological character: first the age of the senses, then the age of great sentiments, and at last the age of reason. Evolution is also of a physical character: this was understood by Vico before the advent of Darwin. The human body modifies itself: the "*human beasts*" become modern man. The Polyphemus-like men with their huge bodies, robust limbs and scarce faculty of reason, evolve, becoming more rational human beings as time goes on. Polyphemus of the Homeric poems is a trace of this, a memory at an almost unconscious level of how men were in a different historical epoch, of how we ourselves were at the dawn of civilisation and that we have almost totally forgotten. The search for these traces (which we can find particularly in myths) can be compared – at a collective level- to what happens in the study of dreams and of our psychological subconscious, according to Freud and his theories. Homer's Poliphemus, the giants of mythology, the Goliaht of the Bible and the giants before the deluge are traces of these human beasts.

The Germanic and Gaul tribes, of whom Caesar and Tacitus speak of more than two millennia ago, were tall and not as rational as the Romans, the former being capable of barbaric fury especially in battle. These Germanic barbarians were to become more humane and rational in successive epochs.

Vico's geographical and ethnographical knowledge is limited if compared to what we know today, but also with respect to what Hegel knew a century later. Vico uses the term *"conjecture"* in his yearning to know more than is possible in the environment in which he lives in the first half of the eighteenth century. He questions himself on what the Patagonian savages are like, physically and psychologically, promising himself to get information on this topic from missionaries who have travelled to those distant regions of the globe, in settings that are far from the civilisation to which he belongs, in order to verify his conjectures.

Vico the humanist knows history of law, besides mathematics and the sciences of his time. His outlook towards the facts regarding the civilisation of the ancient world – comparing it to the modern one of his time – is that of a rational eighteenth century man, humanist and post-humanist if we can define him thus – that is, of a man of science, an anthropologist who keeps in mind man as a whole, who creates poetry and art at first and then the sciences. A man who acknowledges his own creation of a *Scienza Nuova* or new science, that is to say the science of man: sociology. The title of his main work is significant for his consciousness and for his proud stand.

A scientist of the eighteenth century and Vico's contemporary, Anton Lazzaro Moro (1687 – 1764), was similar to him in his attitude towards information on the ancient world which he parallels to his age. He collects shell fossils in the mountains, observes volcanoes, and collects information on the island of Santorini in Greece which had risen following earthquakes and volcanic eruptions in an ancient epoch. He puts together all his information and, through intuition, formulates hypothesis and theories that are the foundation of modern geology. Moro's attitude, like that of Vico, towards information that comes from ancient times is at a different level of knowledge; much more scientific and rational, almost detached with respect to what was the attitude of Machiavelli and the humanists of the fifteenth and sixteenth centuries who saw their reflection in ancient men: men whom they admired and whom they wanted to imitate because the humanists felt a new need to overcome the concepts of their epoch, of their recent past, of the Medieval age which for them was a barbaric epoch. This barbaric epoch was rediscovered and re-evaluated by Vico as an epoch of civility long before the Romantics did so, an epoch which is different from both classical antiquity and his own epoch characterised by greater rationality. Vico's approach was something new: it was a scientific intuition which was to modify the way of understanding the world of man in the same way Darwin's evolution of the species was to modify the understanding of the world of nature.

With reason and genial intuition Vico is interested in the world and in civilisations built by man, in societies which evolve and transform themselves, in the things that men produce: he anticipates, yet is along the same lines as nineteenth century philosophy. He was able to be totally understood only in the second half of the twentieth century when his critics could go beyond even the positive evaluation of the critic Benedetto Croce. It matters little that he is neglected. Despite the formal imperfections and lack of clarity in his writings, his badly expressed concepts, and despite the fact that it is difficult for the reader to sieve through and purify his style and his contents from his waste, we can consider him the forerunner of many *"human sciences"*: anthropology in general, modern linguistics, aestheticism, philosophy of law, philosophy of religions, of man seen globally in all his manifestations of man-creator. A recently published book that had success and that has been appreciated even by Noam Chomsky, <u>The Language Instinct</u>, by Steven Pinker, (William Morrow and Co. Inc., New York, 1994) deals with languages and instinct in learning and never mentions or quotes Vico. It speaks of the evolution of languages but underlines only the technical and mechanical aspects, as could be right and appropriate for a scholastic text that is more specific than this one. This text never deals with the evolution from a poetic language to prose to a more scientific language; it does not mention language as a product and creation of man. Consequently man is not considered in this totalising and omnicomprehensive humanistic dimension and hence, this book, which claims to affront a totalising human topic like linguistic instinct, is a technically limited study. This is the characteristic of many sociological studies that believe they are scientific, yet do not consider man in this more complete dimension. This is the characteristic of many schools in our Western world that aim at educating man in an almost exclusively technological sense, not a complete man in whom a technical and scientific formation is certainly one integral part of his human formation.

This essay on G.B. Vico was intended more to popularise his ideas, his intuitions, his concept of knowledge, particularly the evolution of man throughout history, rather than remain an original contribution to his philosophy. This work is referred especially to American university students and to all those who are interested in history, even modern history in a more global and omnicomprehensive way, and not merely those who are interested in philosophical studies. This paper sometimes underlines a historical political situation of our contemporary world – historical parallels – that brings us towards the understanding of the facts and situations in a world that goes beyond mere registration of facts, or the common way we understand and illustrate them – as happens so often in newspapers and magazines of political nature, or even in history books used in schools. From my personal point of view a noteworthy example is my anticipation of the historical events in the Russia of 1989 and the years that follow. This anticipation or prediction of what was to become a page in human history, was contained in an essay called _L'Occidente,_ published first in 1984 and then in 1987, with arguments such as:

…political institutions should evolve towards more democratic forms of life, the iron hand of dictatorship should evolve and be surpassed with Russia losing part of its military and political prestige in the world…

If this topic in itself is not typical of Vico, being almost a strain on his philosophy, it is at least one way of considering contemporary history with particular mental categories – formed in Vico's knowledge; a knowledge of human societies which evolve according to patterns: societies can differ from one another, with their own personality at the collective level, but they are similar as every single man is similar although he differs from other men in personal character.

Another aspect of history and of life in the contemporary world which interests me in particular, keeping in line with the knowledge and viewpoint of Vico, is the growth and evolution of societies outside the Western world – that can substantially change the present cultural and political predominance on this Earth. We are living in a relatively tranquil period of peace and of material well-being in our late twentieth century Western world, and perhaps we are unaware that evolution and growth – not just economic – of other populations in other continents can be more unstabilising for world peace and cohabitation than was the difficult political relationship between the United States and the Soviet Union some years ago. Russia was and is part of Western civilisation. A pattern of the evolution of humanity which is not of Vico but which I would like to consider with reference to his concept of evolution in phases or stages, is the high birth rate in developing countries or civilisations and of the low birth rate of all countries of our Western world, the latter destined to weaken and die.

Verum Ipsum Factum – the truth is fact – man knows what he makes, man cannot know "*per causas*", with knowledge of cause, that which he has not done. The evidence itself, to our eyes, to our reason, is not a guarantee of perfect or complete knowledge. That which is self-evident may not be incorrect but it is not necessarily the whole truth, it is not knowledge "*per causas*". For Vico it is "*certum*" (sure) and not "*verum*" (true): *certum* can be an aspect of truth, of knowledge, partial knowledge. This is consciousness, the knowledge of the external observer, of the external world. The deductive method of the Cartesians, as the absolute method that reveals knowledge, is condemned. Man cannot know nature *per causas* because he did not create it. God can know nature because he created it. In the book of <u>Genesis</u>, God creates Man, but Man is a special creature made in his image, similar to him: God puts him in a garden and it seems as though He makes man a participant of creation. In this sense he does something, he creates something: he can therefore know *per causas* that which he himself makes. Man can understand mathematics because he himself created it; and he can understand his history in particular because history is made by men, not the understanding of man in itself – but in that which he has created: his history, his actions. With this principle Vico goes far beyond Cartesius's *cogito ergo sum* which is the foundation of all European Enlightenment philosophy which continues far that whole century despite Vico, and in all our modern philosophy to the present day. This principle of knowledge *per causas* was typical Medieval Scholastic philosophy, for which only God could understand the physical world because he himself had created it; and was continued in the fifteenth and sixteenth centuries by the Humanists: by Manetti, Pico, Campanella, and by Bacon – one of Vico's favourite writers, "…Cities, houses, paintings and sculptures, arts and sciences, language and literature – are all things that belong to us, created by us…" said Manetti in 1452. Pico and Ficino had spoken about the independence of man. However, Vico makes this concept his own adding new vigour to this principle by applying it to the history of man, created by man. This is certainly a novelty. However, Vico's most daring contribution is the intuition that there does not exist a static, clear universal and eternal truth, or knowledge. Yet the truth – knowledge *per causas*, is a social process in perennial evolution.

Man is endowed with imagination: man is able to reconstruct through imagination that which he has done or suffered: his hopes, his fears, his desires, his works – both his own and those of his fellowmen. His experience is entwined with that of others, his contemporaries and his ancestors: their works, their monuments, laws, customs and, above all, their language – they still speak to him. Communicating with other men – contemporaries and men of past, understanding them and understanding their symbols and language, is why men form societies and become men in the highest sense of the word. Tacitus and Machiavelli liked reliving the passions of famous historical people whom they described like artists. Lucretius described the ferocious and beastly beginnings of the first men. Bacon and Hobbes perceived the importance of imagination in the creation of myths, and also in forms of civil life. Vico assembles these elements and combines them in a very personal energetic and organic whole in his concept of knowledge *per causas*, of imaginary reconstruction, or of the evolution of humanity in stages – from the stage of wilderness to that of pure reason. He relives the passions of primitive men and at the same time reflects on their state with a detached mentality, more detached, and with other more anthropological argumentation with respect to Machiavelli.

European Enlightenment is an extreme consequence of the Italian Renaissance. Humanism considers man in his completeness, in his totality. The equilibrium of the spirit is its principal characteristic and man's main aim: an equilibrium of reason and sentiment, of body and soul, and the value of man himself as a person faced with nature and God the Almighty. This does not mean total dependency on God as it did in Medieval concepts of Saint Francis of Assisi or Dante, nor does it mean an absolute faith in human reason, as was the extreme concept of the Enlightenment, with an exclusive interest for terrestrial things, in the search for happiness on this earth, with no interest in a religious or transcendental dimension. The Renaissance Humanist is not an atheist. Vico re-evaluates sentiment and what is irrational in man, without holding in contempt the rational aspect as did the first generation of romantics. Vico the rational and energetic humanist returns to the Renaissance concept of the complete man, refusing the excesses of reason and addressing his studies towards man, human sciences, history with more rational, sociological and anthropological argumentation. These excesses of reason would later bring about new myths, new idols or modern ideology, from the Goddess Reason to those of the twentieth century with the lagers and the gulags. Vico tries to impress an energetic sudden turn to those deviations of proud and haughty reason in order to reconduct men of European civilisation towards the more natural limits of their essence of being men, towards an equilibrium of spirit as in the more mature men of Renaissance Humanism.

One of his so-called *degnità* or considerations worthy of note states: *"Men first feel without perceiving, then they perceive with a troubled and moved soul, and finally they meditate with a pure mind, with pure reason"*. The different behaviour of men in different periods reflects the three different stages in the evolution of humanity: with different manifestations in the political institutions, in the production of myths and religions, poetry, art and, in the last stage, philosophy and sciences. Vico shows a cultural preparation which is certainly of a philosophical and literary foundation; but his knowledge and interest for the sciences appears noteworthy: he speaks with expertise of about mineral salts and the magnetic needle which is placed parallel to the Earth's axis (*Autobiografia*). However, Vico turns his interest towards the human world above all else: he creates a new science, an attempt to create or capture a science of the history of men.

The first age is the age of the senses. Men are endowed with little reason and with robust senses. This is an age of the Polyphemus-like men, or human beasts, of the imaginative creation of myths and religious divinities. The second age is that of great sentiments or feelings. Men are endowed with great feeling and imagination. This is the age of heroes and poetry. Men are poets. Language is poetic. The third age is characterised by reason. Men reflect with a pure mind. Language changes from poetic to rational, to the prose. The verse before the prose. After this stage of pure reason, after this historical course, humanity seems to undergo a process of involution and of barbarisation, and we have a recurrence: the beginning of another historical course beginning with another stage or phase. This new cycle, this historical recurrence, begins from a more advanced position with respect to the preceding cycle, hence in history there is progress. And above all the history of men there is the work of Providence which acts both internally and beyond the will of men. This is not a cyclic return without progress and perspectives, as is history for the Greeks. Vico has in mind the course of history of ancient Greece and Rome, and the recurrence of modern history from the Medieval age to his day. In his considerations, Vico completely avoids Hebraic history because it is sacred history with the direct intervention of God; and as far as other civilisations are concerned his knowledge of them is indirect or limited, trusting presumptions and showing his desire to verify in the future. Moreover, regarding the time lapse of evolution of various civilisations, although he maintains himself in the traditional scheme of six thousand years from creation according to the calculations of the Bible and according to the belief of his time, he often refers to *"very ancient times"*, to *"exterminated antiquity"*, and seems to express some doubt with statements of the type: *"...and if we were to consider the origins of the world as do the Chinese ..."*. Vico has an inkling that the history of the world and of the men is more ancient and, hence, longer than what the culture of his time was willing to admit – basing itself essentially on calculations of the stories of the Bible taken literally.

Three different types of civil institutions correspond to these three ages: law, languages and spiritual manifestations. The latter can be poetic and artistic creation on one hand, philosophy and sciences on the other. Although he was interested in the history of men in totality, Vico was mostly interested in the history in the more primitive periods of mankind, in the *"human beasts"*, in the creation of poetry, in Homer: and, in the new barbarism of the Medieval age, in the poetry of Dante. In eighteenth century, the Age of Enlightenment, of reason, we can notice that Dante was less admired as he was considered too irrational and barbaric. Vico (and the romantics in a later epoch) will re-evaluate the poetry of Dante and the Medieval age as an epoch of civility. Shakespeare (who Vico does not know) and the Medieval poets will be re-evaluated in the Romantic epoch.

In a very primitive stage men create religions, says Vico. They create myths, together with – and before – poetry. As the child speaks with animals and animates objects with which he plays, so do primitive men animate nature and create myths and gods. Vico is interested in the religion of the Greeks, in myths, and notices that the language directly reflects the images of gods and myths. In the course of time, with evolution, in the myths told like fables and in the language there remain traces which for most men in the following more rational epochs are no longer of any value: certain forms of language are impossible to understand, certain metaphors are obsolete, men no longer believe in the gods of the Olympus. Yet Vico notices that the primitive men that had created those myths and those fables were convinced of them, of their gods, of their myths, and their metaphors were their most sincere and passionate way of expressing themselves. Men of the later stage, that of pure reason, have another way of expressing themselves – prose, a rational and scientific language, and no longer a poetic language – having different forms of social life. It is no longer Medieval Feudalism or Homeric heroes, but the primitive stage is a necessary stage. There could not be a stage of pure reason if first in that same cultural environment, in that same civilisation, there were not the barbaric stage and that of the imagination with the creation of myths and religions. Much in the same way a mature and rational man would not be thus if he had not first undergone the stages of imagination and feeling in childhood and adolescence.

At this point in this essay some considerations of a general character become necessary. If poetry on one hand and philosophy and science on the other are human creations, things made by men at one or the other moment of their spiritual and psychological evolution are both necessary. Today we cannot state that science is good and useful whereas poetry and irrational things like religion and superstition are not good and useful. Yet both science and technology are things created by men: at a successive moment in history, in the evolution of a civilisation, with respect to the moment of poetry. There would not be science in a human environment, let's say in our Western world, if in preceding epochs there had not been poetry. St. Francis and Dante come before Galileo. Shakespeare comes before Newton. The science and technology of the eighteenth century, the century of the Enlightenment, of reason, are created by men in the same cultural milieu where in the preceding epoch men whose behaviour was not very rational, like the Puritans in England and in America, had created poetry. There is genius, sometimes, in the irrational behaviour of terrorists in developing countries, (an early stage in their evolution) in countries which count more today on the world political scene: these people having self-confidence and faith in the social group to which they belong.

Science and technology, creations of man, are not created in the desert or in immature or not predisposed settings that follow a long spiritual evolution. If the individual man is a complete unity, then a civilisation must show the same characteristics: a man, or civilisation, do not produce poetry alone or science alone in a certain moment of their evolution: but one aspect prevails on the other at a certain moment.

Men create religions, they animate nature with their imagination, they create myths and believe in them – stated Vico a century before Feuerbach would state that God is a creation of man, a sublimation of his feelings.

At a personal level, Vico remains a simple commoner who, despite demonstrating such robust thoughts, remains a believer, a Catholic in the most traditional sense – affirms Benedetto Croce in his important essay on Vico of 1911. Vico is interested particularly in the creation of myths in the Greek world in the Homeric epoch, a primitive epoch, in fact, that created the great poetry of Homer. He shows no interest in studying Christianity, just as he avoided taking an interest in the history of the Hebrews and in relation to other primitive populations. For the modern man Vico's eventual and indirect contribution, even regarding the study of the Bible, could be, in fact, the contribution of a general character regarding the knowledge of language and human speech, literary genres and the essentially poetic images in history, including the history of the Hebrews. His position of the simple believer faced with the history of men to which he himself has contributed for a better understanding of it, is similar to that of the nuclear physicist of our time who contributes to the understanding of nature and of the universe, yet continues believing in Jesus Christ, son of God the Almighty Father, dead and resurrected, as do the more simple men of this Earth.

Two other considerations must be made as a footnote to this concept in which, during a primitive stage in the evolution of mankind, there is the creation of myths, superstitions, religions and poetry. In the same way that primitive people animate nature, talk to animals and consider a tree as a divinity, children also tend to animate the objects they play with and they also talk to the animals. Children are also irrational and are endowed with creative imagination: they are poets like the primitive men. Vico himself in efficient passages of his *Scienza Nuova* (Book I) indicates this fact as a particular characteristic: the poetic language can be used in the education of children. To make the most of the feeling and imagination of children for a didactic aim – in an energetic way and long before J.J. Rousseau was to express similar concepts in his *Emile*. Again, religion is also, and above all, feeling. It is a manifestation and expression of humanity in a primitive stage of the evolution of men. Giovanni Gentile, a non-believer and philosopher of Italian Neo-Idealism, Minister of Public Education in 1923, introduces in his Scholastic Programmes the study of the Catholic religion with this particular view: religion is creation and manifestation of humanity, as is poetry: it is popular philosophy – for a population that is not yet mature. In a successive epoch when humanity will have evolved, there will no longer be need for religion – the latter will be substituted by philosophy, by pure reason. Besides this fact, besides the human and scholastic values themselves, we cannot understand our history if we cannot understand this essential component of our civilisation. In 1929, after the pact between the Italian government and the Holy See, the teaching of religion would be put in the hands of the Catholic Church.

As a second consideration, we must note the quasi-concurrence of the creation of myths, of religions with poetry; we must also note a strengthening in the moral sense. In the Homeric epoch we can notice how images, general language and simple words, belief in myths and divinities, rites and religious practices – were all one, much more connected to one another, intertwined, much more than can appear to men of a successive epoch when men are more rational and can no longer grasp the meaning and the language. In the creation of myths and religions we have a strengthening in the moral and religious sense, and the creation of local religions, of divinities of a particular place, of sects and variations inside a larger complex of beliefs, of particular religious orders. At the beginning of this new historical course of the modern epoch, in the Medieval age, together with and before the flowering of the poetry of the Troubadours in southern France, we have a moral strengthening that is manifested with various heresies: we are not interested in dealing with orthodoxy in this essay but we are interested in dealing with the moral and religious strengthening that is expressed with irrational manifestations. The figure of St. Francis of Assisi in Italy – a poet and a moral figure – is one of great importance in the history of modern Western Civilisation as seen in Vico's omnicomprehensive way. This essay is not interested in discussing whether the Albigenses in southern France, or Francis of Assisi soon after, were or not orthodox; what is sure is that inside this civilisation and inside the dominant religion of its time, they bring something new, something local, some variations to the behaviour of other religious orders and institutions. As a poet and man of a primitive epoch, of humanity at an infantile or developing stage, we know that St. Francis of Assisi speaks to God the Almighty, but also to the earth, to the water, to the birds and to the wolf of Gubbio. St Francis is a Vico-type hero – as Erich Auerbach liked to underline in his essays on Romance Philology.

There still exist the problem of transcendence. Vico accepts the Christian idea of history: above all actions and human suffering – the hand of God guides men towards inscrutable ends that they cannot understand. This action of God above all men is at the same time transcendental and immanent: Vico gives some examples that for us have nothing of the transcendental – as the evolution in stages, for example, and certain immigrations that put different peoples in contact with each other. The same facts and the same actions can be judged by modern rational men in a critical way, even by students of Vico's philosophy, as they want it to be according to their sensibility and their ability to understand the things of mankind like history. One can accept or reject the concept of Transcendental Providence, or consider it immanent, something like Hegel's Idea, and Vico's whole theory holds water in any case. As scholars, as rational men, it may be better not to accept it on its terms. However, at least Vico does not neglect, contrary to other modern philosophers, and especially does not reject the presence of God, or Providence, in history or above the history of men. Franco Amerio and other catholic scholars stress the fact that the scientific discoveries of Vico in the science of man, in the evolution, in the concept of knowledge, get perfectly along with a Christian conception of life. A fact that could be fully understood only late in the twentieth century.

For me it is easier and clearer to understand history through the eyes of Vico when he states that men evolve from a state of human beasts to that of rational men, and that in different periods they create languages, arts, religions, sciences, material things and civil institutions – easier and clearer than other philosophers (who are just as interesting) who state that the *idea materialises in history* (Hegel) through argumentation in the form of *thesis antithesis and synthesis*. Furthermore, Vico's concept is not less materialistic than that of other philosophers: I would say it is more concrete. Yet in this concreteness, in this materiality of the things of man, Vico leaves a small opening for the transcendence – to someone or something that is not of the same substance as the things of man – and at the same time to the transcendent and immanent God of the Christian tradition in which he himself believes with the heart of a commoner in his city, his Naples, in the early eighteenth century, when the men of his time were beginning to become too haughty and proud of their science, reason and of their success, and were beginning to create modern ideologies: evil idols and ideologies created by them and which they believed, in the same way more sincere and spontaneous primitive men had done in preceding epochs by creating myths, superstition, divinities and religions.

YOUSSEF COURBAGE - EMMANUEL TODD
Le Rendez- vous des civilisations
Editions du Seuil et de La republique des Idées, septembre 2007

With this same title it seems that the authors wish to contest the publication *Clash of Civilisations* by Samuel Huntington. The *Clash of Civilisations* has been criticised by Asians, Indians and Chinese alike as the work of a westerner who is competent when he writes about the Western Civilisation, less so when he treats the Asian cultures, with which he is not so well-acquainted. The Indians consider Hegel himself a racist philosopher. *Le Rendez-Vous des Civilisations* shows better understanding of Asians at the present time, with accurate statistic data regarding the various populations. It seems less western orientated, less fearful of the democratic and economic growth of those populations in a phase of development.

Le Rendez- Vous des Civilisations does not take into account the ancient history of the various populations, of their evolution through the ages. The authors seem to be more open, better disposed towards people belonging to diverse cultures; they see the positive aspects of these different civilisations and do not seem to worry too much about the more violent aspects of the others, about terrorism and suicide bombers, about the conditions of women, who, they contend, are treated well in Muslim families. They have faith in the future of these developing populations. They are not aware of the sense of superiority felt by Indians, Chinese and Arabs towards the imperialistic West and their corrupt customs. When illiteracy no longer exists in the world, especially illiteracy among women, they, too, will be able to enjoy improved social services and a sounder economy. All the peoples seem to be heading in this direction, also and especially those belonging to the Muslim religion. In the western countries we were able to enjoy this social and economic progress before the others, from the time we managed to control our birth rate. In former more irrational and more religious epochs – religious referring to any religion - man's fertility was not controlled. Indeed, all religions more or less openly, encouraged a high birth-rate. People were superstitious and irrational, to the disadvantage of everyone. All religions, Christians and Muslims included, in the long run tend to evolve and their irrational attitudes, together with their position in favour of maximum fertility, weaken.

The vertiginous increase in the populations of developing countries in the 60's and 70's of the last century seems to be diminishing, even in the Muslim countries. Islam in itself, more than Christianity, would be more tolerant in matters of fecundity and more indulgent in those regarding sexuality, or better towards the directives of a dogmatic and unrealistic (*dogmatique et irréaliste* - chapter 7) Vatican. A decisive factor, according to the authors is that of education, first of all that of males and then and especially, that of females. Where the education among females reaches 50%, we notice an immediate fall in the birth rate, together with a parallel weakening of religious practice, considered by the authors a positive factor in the march of progress: this is true of every country in the world, beginning with France in the 18th century, continuing with Japan and China at the beginning of the 20th century and the Muslim countries in more recent decades. Some more backward countries in Africa will get there later. The education of females, in some way, lies at the base of birth control, as is demonstrated by statistics in this regard.

A high birth rate seems to constitute a negative factor as regards economic growth. The father of a family with too many children will not be able to feed and educate all of them. If he controlled his fecundity, he would be better able to look after himself and his children. Even if he worked hard and was a positive element in the community, too many children would be an impediment to him, a burden which would prevent him, and his family, from reaching self- fulfilment in both the economic and the social sense. Preventive birth-control or the death of some of his children, would be a positive factor in this direction.

I am fully sympathetic with this kind of situation.

My position regarding the matter as compared to that of the authors Youssef Courbage and Emmanuel Todd is similar to that of G.B. Vico's philosophy on history compared to the philosophy of the Enlightenment. The philosophy of the Enlightenment must not be considered entirely incorrect, just as the position of the two authors is not to be considered incorrect but, rather, limited, relating to a limited or partial truth. They give a picture of an actual situation, of an evolution covering little more than a century, of a situation in which education, first of all for males and in a second moment for females, lies at the base of an epoch- making change. When education touches at least 50% of the population, or at least 50% of women between the ages of 20 and 24, the first effects of a desired birth control become apparent, as does the change from both the social and the economic points of view which the two authors – and many other experts in the world, including those at the United Nations – aspired to.

The philosophers of the Enlightenment did not like the past, they did not like the dark ages dominated by irrationality and superstition, they did not like the Middle Ages. All peoples are the same: education can do all the good in the world. The philosophers of the Enlightenment wanted to change the world through man's capacity to reason; they wanted to search for happiness, they wanted to bring about happiness on Earth using their faculty of reasoning. They did not want to hold to account that dark ages too form an integral part of the history of humanity, of the whole life of mankind. They did not want to hold to account that in the dark ages too man had achieved great things. They did not consider the fact that the rationalism of the enlightened years was only a moment, a significant moment certainly but a phase in the evolution of civilisation. When we have a problem, affirmed the rationalists of the 18th century following in the footsteps of René Descartes, and modern thinkers also, we examine it from all points of view. We check and test every aspect of a particular question and, in the end, that which appears clear and distinct to us, that is the truth. Vico would say that that is not the truth, that is *certum*, not *verum*, that is to say, that is a partial truth, not a truth *per causas*. The history of mankind must be considered from all its aspects, including the dark years of our Middle Ages during which irrationality and superstition reigned overall, affirmed Vico, including those times when *"men perceive the world around them with a disturbed and emotional soul"* (consider today's suicide bombers and terrorists, the extreme aggression and fanaticism throughout the ages), including the periods in which *"men reflect with a pure mind"*. Consider the creators of science and technology today and in the recent past.

I ask myself if birth control too should be intended in the inverse sense. Fascism in Italy and Nazism in Germany encouraged large families and a high birth rate for reasons of national prestige: to have more youths for the Armed Services, more strength in general and a larger labour force. These ideals differed from those of the post Second World War period and in these years astride the two millenniums, at least in the western world. The leaders of the former period aspired to conquering the world, they had faith in their own peoples, in progress, and birth control moved in the opposite direction to that of today inasmuch as we Europeans no longer aim at conquering the world and carrying ahead our mission of civilising the others. We no longer are overconfident. We simply wish to enjoy life, with a thriving economy and efficient social services. France experienced a fall in the birth rate before the other European nations and tried to get round the problem by promoting the emigration of Italians, Spanish, Poles and later people from the African colonies. The problem lay in France's fear of Germany. She needed more young forces to defend her against the aggression of her enemy. Family benefits encouraging large families, and immigration both worked towards this end. Birth control acts inversely for different reasons and different ideals.

The two authors also state that that it is interesting to see that when a population is numerically inferior to other dominant populations around them, an unconscious way of defending itself is to increase demographic growth. This is the case of the Muslims in Europe who actually declare openly that they want to generate many offspring in order to drive out the Europeans from Europe and take their place. It is the case of the Albanians in Kossovo in the face of the threatening Serbians. It is also the case of Lebanon and Malaya, faced with an ever-increasing number of Chinese and Indian immigrants, and of other ethnic minorities in other developing countries.

The authors do not take into consideration the fact that in times past, in other civilisations, in other contexts, these phenomena manifested themselves in a similar way even when education, be it of males or females, did not come into the question. Another fact belonging to the distant past but which repeats itself also today, is that civilisations tend to die out completely, or almost, in the long run. They sometimes leave traces – more or less important – of their cultural heritage. Death forms part of the life of each person, and in a like manner in the life of all civilisations. Death means the end of a civilisation, an end which may be brought about for diverse reasons: a tragic war, a fatal disease or a particularly adverse fate, but if it reaches its full maturity, the end of a civilisation is pre-announced by a decline in its fertility.

In my opinion, birth control, both in one sense and in the other is an induced factor, important but secondary. I use the term *induced* with respect to the fact that over the ages high and low birth rates are natural phenomena which have manifested themselves several times throughout history, in the long periods of evolution of civilisation. Improved medical knowledge and improved methods of agriculture certainly favour demographic growth, but they themselves are induced phenomena, almost secondary with respect to the natural pattern of the growth and decline of civilisations over a long period of time. Control of the fertility using contraceptive medicines is another induced, almost secondary phenomenon. In Europe and in the Western World in general, the birth rate would have fallen anyway during the last two generations, even without the various campaigns for birth control. It could be eventually a moral aspect, which I do not wish to take into consideration. My theory seems to be diametrically opposed to that of the two French authors Youssef Courbage and Emmanuel Todd:

The whole of humanity, or a particular civilisation, or even a social class, a population, progresses when the birth rate is high: scientific, technological and economic progress and the conquest of lands included. It regresses and loses its scientific and technological knowledge before disappearing from the face of the Earth when its birth rate is low and when its vital energy weakens and dies.

The vision of the two French authors, rather than incorrect seems rather limited to me. Human life and the history of mankind are to be considered in their entirety, from birth to death. The authors take into consideration only a limited period of the long evolution of civilisation: the moment in which at the present time the education of the masses leads to a more rational vision of life and to an improvement in living conditions. An interesting moment with particular characteristics which have manifested themselves in a similar manner in other historical contexts, in other past civilisations which have since disappeared. They seem to ignore completely the irrational factor and the aggressive character of many populations undergoing a phase of development – a very important irrational factor which lies at the base of an intensive development.

THE INDIAN CIVILIZATION AND THE WESTERN CIVILIZATION AS PARALLELS

The whole history of India may be considered in parallel to the history of Europe, the modern western civilization, the antique Greek and Roman civilizations and the civilization of the Middle East. There are differences, as is only natural but there are also some surprising parallels.

The civilization which grew around the valley of the Indus had its beginnings towards 3000 BC and covered an area of more than one million square kilometers. It lasted until towards 1600 BC when other populations began to arrive, Indo-Europeans bringing with them another type of civilization and the Sanskrit language and culture. It seems that it was not these new populations coming from the north west, from Iran, from the Caucasus and the Russian plains, who brought about the decadence and the end of the Harappa civilization. This would have happened anyway, for internal causes which have not yet been fully understood, - or perhaps they have. The decline and fall of that great civilization would have been brought about by natural causes after its growth and its maximum expression, by the natural exhaustion of its vital energy thrust, as has happened to all civilizations throughout the course of history.

Unlike the contemporary civilizations in Mesopotamia with which the Indus Valley civilization seemed to have had contact and relations, we have not been able to understand the writings. We know many things about those populations living in the fertile region situated between the rivers Tigris and Euphrates, and about Egypt; we know that they were Semites, we know how they were organized, their epic poems, their religion, their laws and codes, their level of technology and their types of civil constructions. The most important political and cultural centres of the civilization varied geographically over the territory; the most important town was sometimes in the north, sometimes in the south, depending on the stage of maturity reached and on the luck of the single peoples belonging to this civilization, on the organization of their political entities. As far as the

Indus Valley is concerned we know only the level of technology reached, the fact that they too were excellent farmers and that they produced a surplus of agricultural food products, which favoured the organization of life in the towns, and that they dug irrigation channels – as in Mesopotamia. We know relatively little about their religion: that which we know we deduce from the sculptures, the stamps and the seals which have survived, not from written texts which we manage to find, but which do not speak to us. We know that the peoples of the Middle East were Semites – the Hebrews are one of the Semite populations closely linked for their type of civilization, but other peoples of the same region were not, like the Hittites in Asia Minor who were Indo Europeans, and the Sumerians, the first people we are going to take into consideration for having introduced writing and a type of modern agriculture and political organization and in the course of time seem to have disappeared and been assimilated into successive populations in Mesopotamia. We do not know who these Sumerians were, to which branch or human race they belonged, just as we do not know who the inhabitants of the Indus Valley were. We can suppose that they were rather dark-skinned peoples like the very first inhabitants of Crete and that in some way the Tamil populations of modern day India are related to them. This civilization of the Indo Valley can be compared in everything to the whole civilization of Mesopotamia, only that we do not know exactly what spiritual, technological and religious inheritance has been passed on to successive generations. Probably this inheritance is notable, but we cannot measure it as we can, on the other hand, that of the Akkadian populations of Mesopotamia to the Hebrews and the Greeks.

Modern day India is made up principally of two anthropological groups more or less intermingled, the Indo Europeans to the north and the Tamils to the south, with two main language groups, while other populations, numerically smaller and with language groups which are completely different, are scattered over the territory in small populations, which became more isolated after the Arian invasions. The Arian invasions into the territories of the former civilization of the Indus Valley, first of all, and then later towards the east and the south of India, took place over a very long time in at least two principal waves lasting for a period of more than one thousand years each. A little like the Germanic invasions of the territories of the Roman Empire beginning before Marius and Caesar and continuing until after Charles the Great. Or again like the first wave of Indo European migrations towards Europe coming from the east, from the Russian plains and the Caucasus, in the second millennium BC, parallel to and contemporary with the first Indo-European invasions in India. Like the Doric migrations in the Hellenic world in 1000 BC in the Minoan civilization of Greece. The Indian experts today insist on the fact that the word Arian means war lords, nobles, and has no connotations with racialism. The same word we find in reference to the geographical names of Haryana (a state to the north of Delhi), Iran (Persia) and of Eire (Ireland, Celtic Indo-European). The sense of racial superiority conferred upon it by modern European ideologies seems to be pure mystification, a demented degeneration which has caused a lot of pain and incomprehension.

The level of technological knowledge possessed by the civilization in the Indus Valley was certainly superior to that of the Indo-European populations who were arriving in India towards the middle of the second millennium BC, just as the populations of the Roman Empire had reached a superior level as respect that of the barbaric Germanic peoples coming from the north and the east. But the latter were in that particular phase of their history, of their evolution, in which the vital energy of populations undergoing a stage of development is manifest: we are at the beginning of a new phase of civilization.

The Arians who began to arrive in India in the middle of the second millennium BC possessed a language similar to contemporary European languages, in particular to Latin and Greek. They are presumed to belong to the same ethnic group, with those understandable differences which several millenniums can produce. Recently, in India controversies have arisen concerning the actual identities of these Indo-Arian populations coming from the north west and the impact that these new civilizations could have had on the previous populations already there. It has even been suggested that these new populations were in fact aboriginals, Indians, and that from India they had moved north-west, towards the Caucasian plains and towards Europe. This supposition seems to me to be an extreme position on the part of the Indian National parties. There are certain professors of history who have been threatened because they refuse to accept this theory, because they have taken on a position which is too close to European conceptions, linked themselves to a colonial, anti-Indian mentality. This does not seem to me to be a correct attitude. In Europe too, in other historical periods, we have experienced cases in which a certain ideology has risked deforming the historical truth and seeing there only what we want to see.

It is far more interesting to see how this new Arian civilization influenced and, in its turn was influenced by the former civilizations: in technology, in religion, in language, just like the Germanic tribes of barbarians when they arrived in the territories of the Roman Empire they had invaded. Certain divinities of the Hindu pantheon do not seem to exist in the more antique sacred texts, those written before their arrival in Indian territories, and seemingly were incorporated after their arrival, influenced by other pre-existent religions. It also appears that the Arians, with their military organization, were not such able farmers as those dwelling in the Indus Valley, but were familiar with horses trained for combat and perhaps even reared them. In the seals and in the small amount of iconography which we manage to obtain from the remains of the Indus Valley Civilization which have survived, we are able to identify the cow and the plough, not the horse which seems to have been introduced by the Arians.

One of the elements of particular interest as regards the Arian civilization is the impact of the same on India, and the parallel we can make with the ancient western civilization, with the Greek civilization and with Sanskrit literature: the Vedas first of all, all the epic poetry of the Mahabhrarata and the Ramayana, in parallel with the poetry of Homer. The Vedas consists of around a thousand sacred hymns, of a religious character, some of which seem to have been composed before the arrival of the Arians in India, perhaps even before 2000 BC. Such antiquity could be demonstrated by a philological analysis of the texts, of the single words which over a long period of time tend to evolve, as in all languages of the world – in addition to the contents. Experts in Indian studies have also identified references to certain astronomical observations which would date them even earlier, if not the compiling of the hymns, at least the oral composition and the information collected. Some scholars, like the Nobel Prize winner Amartya

Sen, do not agree. And reference is still made to the river Saraswati which it is claimed changed its course in a more westerly direction, as can be seen today by satellite studies on the territory and the southern flow of the river Indus on whose banks some of the towns of the Indus Valley civilization grew up (Dohlavira, Harappa, Mohenjojaro). Other towns can be traced today below sea level, on the south coast of the Sind (today in Pakistan), and of Gujarat.

In the 5000 years of history which we are briefly reviewing India has never been politically united, except under English domination in the 19ᵗʰ and the 20ᵗʰ centuries. However, immediately after India gained her independence, she was once more divided. On the contrary, the Chinese civilization has always been unified under one political centre. Unlike India, China has always tended to organize itself around a centralized state and to absorb, one after the other, all the populations which succeeded in invading and conquering her with their armies. The antique western civilization was united politically for several centuries in the times of the Roman Empire and also, at least in part, with the Sacred Roman Empire of Charles the Great. Not, however, in modern times. Modern western civilization is characterized by a myriad of independent states, as was the Ancient Greek civilization.

Here we are taking into consideration modern day India, that large republic with a thousand million inhabitants, capital city Delhi. But as a region and as Indian civilization, together with India real and proper, we must consider also Pakistan, Bangladesh and Sri Lanka, and at least part of Afghanistan and Indonesia. We must thank the entire epic and religious tradition represented in the Veda for the sense of cultural unity, in the Mahabbrhata, and in the Sanskrit language. This prestigious language is still spoken today by about 50,000 people, the more learned, and was that which Latin was until a short time ago in Europe, a language which has died out as has Greek, but which gave tone to all the culture and well-read persons in Europe, also in the scientific field.

Another element which confers a sense of unity on India today is represented by the English language. All cultured persons and those in the world of business speak English. In Parliament in Delhi English is used for communication. The catholic missionaries speak together in English and in their schools English is taught together with the local languages. In India there are at least twenty main languages, almost all of them derived from or influenced by Sanskrit, and many other minor languages using nine different alphabets in their written forms. The single language most widely spoken in India is Hindi, but its diffusion does not reach 50%. Many people in India resent bitterly the fact that Hindi imposes itself over other minor languages. Before English, Farsi, a prestigious Persian language, was considered the official language in the whole of India. Another element which has given a sense of unity in the history of modern, contemporary India, is the sense of **"Indianness"**, feeling themselves to be Indians both as regards culture and civilization; it is the nationalistic sentiment of independence and rebellion against the English occupation shared by all Indians. The last English viceroys in India (Lord Irving above all) were aware of the fact that the history of men inexorably follows a certain direction – the history of all men on this earth. They understood that England and the whole of Europe were undergoing a phase of complete decadence while India, on the other hand, was re-awakening. Mahatma Gandhi was informed directly of this sentiment by the Viceroys and of this intention on the part of the English: England had been a colonial imperialist power. During her occupation of India she had tried to gain maximum economic profits for herself. But now, after the disastrous Second World War – but also before this, she understood that she could no longer maintain military occupation, and she got ready to leave India in an almost peaceful and friendly manner. She was almost seeking to maintain friendly relations with the Indian civilization, a sense of goodwill and good feelings, one of the more positive aspects of the meeting and intermingling of two or more cultures. She left a railway network in working order, a postal service and democratic forms of government following western models.

In her long history, beginning at least with the arrival of the Arians in Indian territory, India has experienced many forms of government, of political organization, not only an absolute monarchy, or in any case, centralized, with important territorial expansion and an attempt at unification, as in the times of the Mauryas (3rd century BC), of the Guptas (around 400 AD), or more recently of the Moghul Muslims (17th century). In the beginning and before the Arian invasions many small peripheral states, had forms of republican governments.

The greatest man that India has ever had was Buddha. Mahatma Gandhi, they keep repeating in India, was the greatest man born in India after Buddha.

In the period between the VII and the V centuries BC, at least six masters were operating in India whose doctrines varied from an atomism similar to that which was later to become theorized by the Greek Democritus, to the affirmation of principles such as that of the impossibility to know the ultimate truth, to the irrelevance of action, non-violence towards all living creatures, the noble truth of moral feelings and right actions and the principle of reincarnation. Non-violence and reincarnation were new concepts, not included in the religious principles of the Vedas. We have more precise biographical information of at least two of these six maestri, even if it was re-elaborated in the following centuries: Mahavira, founder of Jainism, who died in 468 BC., and Siddharta or Gautama, said The Buddha, around 486 BC. They were both offspring of aristocratic families, of the governing elite of those republics which represented the transitional phase from a tribal society to an absolute monarchy.

Today Buddhism is considered a religion and the Hindus consider Buddhism and Jainism variants in respect to the Hindu tradition. To the more rational eyes of the westerners Buddhism appears to be more a philosophy of life than a real and proper religion with one or more divinities to worship. We can identify in Buddhism the opposition to the almost monotheistic religiosity of the Vedas of all the preceding epoch. We can see the rationalizing ambient in which such a religion develops, together with other contemporary maestri of new religions. We can see that in the seventh and sixth centuries BC in the Indian cultural ambient mathematical intuitions emerge together with the rationality of thought. We cannot prove definitely, but tradition, certain clues, suggest that the famous Greek mathematician Pythagoras (570 -496 BC), who believed in metempsychosis, the transmigration of the soul, was at least influenced by the Indian civilization. Indian scholars today insist on the fact that notable traces of geometrical and mathematical problems are evident in the sacred texts of the Hindu tradition (Amartya Sen does not agree). In any case, it is interesting to note that in this epoch, round about the sixth century BC, the cultural ambient in India is becoming more rational as regards the great ideal ambitions, the irrationality of the poetry and the religiosity of preceding epochs, the epoch of the Vedas, in spite of the greatness of the human values contained in the poetry and the religiosity.

There is an interesting parallel with the Greek world: philosophy, reason, mathematics all belong to a period successive to that of Homer's poetry, to the great epics of the Greek civilization. There is a great sense of religiosity in the Homeric poems, besides the epic poetry. In the successive epoch, more rational in tone, men cast a doubt as to whether the gods on Olympus had really existed. Socrates was condemned to death because he was accused of corrupting the young men, because he was not sufficiently religious. We can see again a singular parallel with the Buddha who cast a doubt over previous religious beliefs, and his philosophy lies at the base of a new religion, perhaps more than he intended it to. In the West too, in Greece, Plato is a moral figure and he himself influenced the moral behavior of many generations of scholars. Later there will be misunderstandings with Christianity itself, in the Fathers of the Church, caused by the Platonic sense of morality - the nature of which could be considered almost religious.

Let us reconsider: poems and Homeric epics for Greece first, in more antique times, then in a successive phase of civilization – reason, philosophy and mathematics. In India: epics and religiosity expressed especially in the Vedas first, and in a second time rationality in the teachings of Buddha and Mahavira and the contemporary creation of mathematics and philosophy. We can consider Buddha a contemporary of Socrates, born about eighty years after the former. We can suppose that certain scientific and technological discoveries, certain cultural points of view could have influenced other geographically distant civilizations in the space of a century or two, even if there is no evidence to prove it beyond the shadow of a doubt.

I would like to propose a third parallel, at least as a provocation, a postulate, a hypothesis which I am not able to prove. Confucius is one of those philosophers who has had an immense success with and influence over another antique civilization in the world: China. Confucius, contemporary of Buddha and almost a contemporary of Socrates, was not the only rational thinker in the China of his time. His moral teachings recall those of Buddha in a more practical sense, more economic, more civilized, less metaphysical: he looks at the world around him, at work, at the economy, in a more concrete way. In every civilization of a certain value, in its evolution, in the patterns which repeat themselves – similar to other civilizations, let them be contemporary or of a different epoch, remains the fact of personality: every civilization, like every single man, has its own personal characteristics, very personal, as is evident when considering the works of art of a single artist or a single civilization. Greek art differs from that of another civilization. So, apart from the particular personality of the Chinese civilization, similar to but at the same time different from others, from the Indian civilization, and those of the western world and Greece, - the epoch of a certain rationalism represented by Confucius, suggests the existence of a preceding epoch, at least several centuries before, one in which epics prevailed, and heroic and religious poetry. This is a postulate, in agreement with Vico's conception of history, for which before the epoch in which men reflect with a pure mind " *men consider the world with a perturbed and emotional soul*". And they create poetry and religions. But I cannot seem to find evidence of an epoch of such dimensions in China at the beginning of the first millennium BC., or before. A friend of mine, a young, brilliant scholar, made an interesting suggestion: it happened in China, shortly before the Han epoch in the third century BC. as happened in other cultural ambients in the west, that the Emperor ordered that all the works of art be burned, with the aim of building a new world centred around reason, following reason and all the philosophical concepts of the moment. In 213 BC., the emperor Ying Zheng of the Qin dynasty, energetic unifier, builder and reformer, ordered that all antique texts be burned, except those of a scientific or technical nature, and he had several men of letters put to death. In Florence Savonarola had books and works of art burned in the town squares, but his reasons were purely moral. The Enlightenment in Europe wanted to get rid of all the works relating to the past - to the Middle Ages, which reflected a religious and obscurant character. Islam burnt the library at Alexandria because from its extremist point of view it was useless and dangerous. Germany under the Nazis burnt the books which the regime did not like or agree with. This burning of books in China in the third century BC could have had consequences politically more radical in the Emperor's intentions. As a result much information about the preceding centuries has been lost.

The Indian civilization in parallel with the antique Greek and Roman civilizations and the modern western world has at least one characteristic which appears different: historiography. In the west we have a tradition of historians of great respect: Herodotus, Xenophon, Tucidides, Polybius, Sallust, Livy, Tacitus, and many others. At times their writings seem to give only information and descriptions of populations and places, descriptions of political or military events; at others there seems to be a true and proper concept of life and of history. The information so obtained shows a certain accuracy on the part of the authors in reporting the facts and commenting on them. The historical books of the Bible are a narration of events but also a particular philosophy of history, with information of a certain accuracy, with reports of even negative facts which other peoples would have left out, and with reflections on the reason for certain behavior and the presence of Man on the Earth. In India such a tradition is lacking. The Arabs have only one philosopher of history who deserves that name: Ibn Khaldun (1332-1406).

An event of particular importance towards understanding the history of India and to give a precise enough date to events is the descent of Alexander The Great in the years 326- 325 BC. The Indian civilization had had some contact first with the civilization of Mesopotamia, then with the Greek world, with reciprocal influences. The influence of India on the Greek world was more evident than vice versa, as seems to be demonstrated by the presence of Pythagoras and the Greek mathematicians, who could have been influenced in some way by the Indian civilization, even if indirectly. With arrival of Alexander, the influence of the Greek civilization in India is notable, as bear witness the new techniques of artistic expression, but more important is the dating of the events and situations and a more modern concept of historic reality. Later, with the arrival of the Arabs and Islam, India would continue to exercise her cultural influence over the western world, as is evident in her contribution to mathematics: the Indians are proud to demonstrate that our so-called *"Arabic"* numbers are really *"Indian"*. The Arabs took them directly from India and then introduced them into Europe.

During the long centuries of the epoch of Alexander up to modern times, India seems to have been at a standstill, a relative stasis, not of profound evolution characterized by radical changes, barbarian invasions an intense Medieval period first, followed by a period of Renaissance as happened in Europe: a renaissance intended in a more ample sense with an Enlightenment seen as an extreme evolution of the Italian Renaissance, and a growth and expansion which was to guide Europe and the western civilization in general to create new sciences and new technologies and to expand and impose itself over the whole world. Up to the time when it exhausted its vital energy thrust at the end of the 20th century. The standard of living remained relatively high in India, if compared with that in Europe itself up to the French Revolution. A notable contribution on the part of India to the creation of mathematics and the astronomic sciences arrived towards the fifth and sixth centuries with Arryabatta (499), Varahmihira (505 – 587), Brahamagupta, Bhaskara and others, shortly before the arrival of the Arabs and Islam, which coincides with a period of stasis and deeper decadence. The Indians knew the form of the earth and its dimensions and they already had a primary meridian in Ujjain a long time before that at Greenwich. We also have an interesting case: the Indian scientific community condemned the theories of Arryabatta just as in Europe the scientific communities – and not just the Church- were to condemn Galileo.

At the end of the 18th century, the city of Calcutta was wealthier and more prosperous than London – as English visitors themselves referred. The level reached as regards technological knowledge was also admirable, in the art of weaving, for example, and not at all inferior to that of contemporary Europe. The visitors, Europeans and Arabs, Marco Polo at the end of the XIII century and Ibn Battuta shortly afterwards describe India and all the Asian countries in positive terms. It was only through their contact with the European colonialists, with the English in particular, with their strife for independence and the retreat of the English, that India gave signs of a profound political and cultural renaissance. The increase in the population is one of the aspects of this vertiginous growth. We can already perceive signs of this new phase before the arrival of the English. Historical recurrence of events – *courses and recourses* – as Vico loved to repeat. The rebellions and the wars to drive the English out of India are called *wars of independence*, like the wars fought by the Italians against the Austrians during the Risorgimento. India, like Italy in the XIX century, wanted to affirm itself after a long period of decadence. India today is a world power.

REFORM IN ENGLAND AND IN ISLAMIC COUNTRIES

A parallel

One only has to watch a documentary on the history of England in the 16th century with King Henry VIII and the Queens, Bloody Mary, Elizabeth and Mary Queen of Scotland to discover a parallel with what is happening now in those countries under Islamic regimes.

Protestant Reformation is a historical phenomenon which took place in Northern Europe at the beginning of the 16th century. It began on the Continent with Luther and Calvin but had its repercussions in England too. The Reformation, doctrinal in itself, was characterised by a strengthening – not always rational - of the moral and religious spirit against Roman Catholicism and against the Pope, and the implications were not only of a religious but also of a political nature. In order to fully understand the historical significance of this phenomenon, in situations which have been repeated many times throughout history, I have adopted the approach of G. B. Vico (1668 – 1744) towards history: *men create religions*. If this expression, *create religions* could appear exaggerated (but it is not), or a little difficult to understand, it is true to say that in certain historical epochs, we can identify an irrational strengthening of the religious and the moral spirit (and also the creation of a poetic language and poetry), with reforms both violent and non-violent (St. Francis) in nature, but always passionate with a *perturbed and emotional spirit*.

This is also a sign of progress: a population which is interested by this phenomenon is itself in an initial phase of its evolution and about to assert itself on the world's political scene, while other more rational populations are on the decline.

England found herself in this delicate initial phase of her evolution towards the conquest of a leading political role in the world at the time of the Protestant Reformation, compared to a more rational and more advanced

Southern Europe with Spain as the politically dominant nation. King Henry VIII adopted the ideas and the examples coming from the Germanic world: the rebellion against the Pope and Rome, and against the power of Spain; he made them his own, to his political advantage. In England and in Scotland we have the emergence of individuals and situations of a religious and a moral nature which recall, to a certain extent, the various Ayotollah in the Islamic world today. Mary Queen of Scotland was bitterly criticised for her "immoral behaviour" (John Knox) just as Ayotollah Khomeini in Iran criticised the habits of the Iranian women who, in his opinion, were too modern. He despised the women in the West (taking as his example the Parisiennes) holding them to be decadent and corrupt. A good parallel could be drawn between Ayatollah Khomeini (1902- 1989) in Iran, and John Calvin (1509 – 1564) in France and Switzerland, both for religious and political – historical motivations.

King Henry gained advantage from the new ideas, anti-Pope and anti - Spain. Queen Mary Tudor thought she could restore law and order and equilibrium to England with energetic policies and the persecution of the hotheads and the Protestants, but her actions did not appear too wise and they were not far-reaching enough. Her sister, Elisabeth, on the other hand, was much more far-sighted and intelligent; she was able to hold her ground. She did not adopt the new ideas and the new examples directly, and she did not directly persecute anyone; she tried to concentrate the whole energy of the nation on its future well-being, independently of religious faith, even if in the end, she, too, proved to be anti-Catholic and anti-Spain. With the same political ability she was able to discuss political and economic questions with Parliament, and hold her own, and she knew how to deal with the most ardent and impetuous men of her time. The Stuart Kings who succeeded her did not have her same ability and far-sightedness, and their internal policy, lacking in insight, led the Puritans to exasperation, to civil war and to the establishment of the Commonwealth. Oliver Cromwell, in fact, himself a Puritan, overthrew the monarchy. He was, nevertheless, to reveal himself to be a politician of exceptional capability; he put the general interest of England first and foremost, before the little-rational religious interests of the same Puritans. A number of Puritans were to leave for the New Continent, America, where they would be able to live freely according to their moral and religious principles. These Puritans, aggressive in character and not very rational, were to become the founders of a new nation, a new civilisation founded on religious and moral bases. Later, the age of religious extremism was to evolve into a period with more rational lifestyles and into the more tolerant atmosphere of the Enlightenment. But in these two centuries, which were fundamental to the history of England, we can distinguish diverse episodes of intolerance, both religious and moral, numerous plots and attacks, and irrational attitudes. Those politicians who were more enlightened knew how to overcome difficult situations and even to gain advantage from them, both at home faced with the more irrational and impetuous members of all the political groups, and abroad, on the seas, when dealing with other dominant world powers, independently of their religious beliefs.

In the Islamic world today we are faced with a situation which is very similar to that in Northern Europe and England after the Protestant Reformation, when men *strengthened their irrational moral and religious spirit,* when men looked at the world with a *perturbed and emotional soul,* when they were growing and asserting themselves in the world, while other more rational populations were in a phase of decline and decadence. The Islamic peoples, too, later – in a few centuries time, or at least, within a few generations, are destined to become more rational and to lose some of that aggressiveness which characterises them today, and, indeed, is also characteristic of those Englishmen who fought against the Spaniards and of the Puritans both in England and on the American Continent who, little by little, became more rational. All the Islamic nations today count for more in the world politically than they did one or two generations ago. The Islamic peoples today are aggressive and arrogant towards the more rational western civilisations, as were the Puritans and the English people in general towards the Catholics and towards Spain, the most powerful nation in the world at that time.

How do politicians in the Muslim countries today behave in front of the phenomenon of extremism? Our information regarding this argument comes from the outside, provided by journalists, and thus we cannot evaluate with precision the political importance of the phenomenon, which should be seen in its particular historical context. We lack, in fact, a temporal historical perspective. However, the general character is very similar to that of the Protestant Reformation in England and in Northern Europe in the 16th and the 17th centuries, at the beginning of a period of progress for those populations. The more specific characteristics are different, as are the arts and other manifestations of every civilisation. The irrational phenomenon of the suicide terrorists is particular to the Islamic extremists today. Another difference can be seen in the fact that, whereas for the peoples of the Christian faith, politics and religion are on two different planes which rarely coincide, for the peoples of the Islamic faith, religion and the political life go hand in hand. (Consider, however, the fact that the Republic of Ireland remains Catholic in political contrast with the dominant Protestant England, and that Poland remains Catholic to distinguish herself from Protestant Germany and Orthodox Russia).

Ibn Khaldun (1332-1406), historian and philosopher, the Arabian Vico, described the religiosity and the irrational, aggressive attitudes of the Berberic tribes and the Arabs at the time of their expansion into Mediterranean territories immediately following the death of Mohammed. Consider also the increase in the population and the fact that the psychological religious factor plays an important part in the Islam religion; it binds and unites all the Arab tribes and directs them towards a common objective. Religion becomes an anthropological and cultural element which contributes to the process of concentrating all the energies of a population on political objectives of a historical character, like the conquest of the world, for example, independently of the intrinsic value of the religion itself, of the pureness of the ideals one lives and fights for. This fact can be easily exploited by those politicians gifted with Machiavellian intelligence: an Ayotollah, for example, or another political Head of State indoctrinates his patriotic young people, promises them paradise with virgins who come to welcome them, and sends them to meet an enemy target with their belts laden with explosives.

Among the various politicians in the Islamic countries at our present time, I am trying to understand, at times to guess, which are the most intelligent, the most far-sighted. There have been attacks not only against western targets, considered as enemies, or against other enemy objectives, in India, for

example, but also against other Heads of States declared openly to be Islam..
A plot in India against Hindu targets, organised and prepared in Pakistan,
was not necessarily the work of the legitimate Pakistan government, but
that of independent rebel forces. Could the legitimate Pakistan government
have profited by such an attack? Here only time will tell. During the stages
of greatest agitation in the Italian Risorgimento, there were terrorist attacks
both inside and outside Italian territory; in France, for example, against
Napoleon III, who took the side of the Italian patriots. It was Cavour, an
exceptional politician, who knew how to gain profit from such difficult and
unpleasant situations. Then there is the episode of Guglielmo Oberdan
in Trieste. He was considered a hero by Italian propaganda during the
Risorgimento, but in the eyes of the Austrian police, who caught him with
a bomb in his hands, he was a terrorist.

Queen Elisabeth took the side of the Protestants, with prudence and
intelligence, and tried to gain advantage from the situation for England,
and not for one sect or another. Oliver Cromwell was himself a Puritan
extremist, gifted with magnanimous ideals, a different Bin Laden. But
Cromwell was intelligent and far-sighted. And in the end it was the general
interest of England which counted more for him than the interests of the
Puritans. Will there be another Bin Laden as intelligent as Cromwell in the
Islamic countries? Or will there be some other head of an Islamic State able
to hold his ground with the irrational hotheads around him, who knows how
to direct all the energy of all these hotheads towards nobler, more concrete
objectives? Or will some other hothead emerge, some other extremist *with
a perturbed and emotional spirit*, who is not very rational and will lead his
people and a great part of humanity to ruin and total destruction? The
history of mankind is made up of many things: life (vitality) and death are
both aspects of human existence on this Earth..

The epoch of the protestant Reformation in Europe and in England was
the first to manifest a phase of great progress, after, and as an extreme
consequence of the Italian Renaissance. Adopting Vico's line of thought, we
can identify first of all this strengthening of the moral and religious spirit
with demonstrations of irrational and aggressive attitudes. We can also note
the creation of poetry, of a poetic language, both in England and in Northern

Europe, and detect a vital surge of energy accompanied by an increase in the population and expansion overseas. This first epoch of great progress precedes a second one during which men *reflect with a pure mind*, the epoch of rationalism, of philosophy, of science; the Age of Enlightenment. In the Islamic world today we can detect the same strengthening of the moral and religious spirit in irrational terms, the intense aggressiveness, the same *vital surge of energy* together with an increase in fertility and in the population numerically. Politically, also, they count more in the world today than they did two generations ago.

We do not know what the near future will bring, but having observed the patterns of evolution of other civilisations in other historical contexts, we can imagine how things will go with a certain amount of accuracy. These Islamic nations should become even more important in the near future. But they are men, they are living creatures on this Earth. Like all the others who have preceded them, they are not destined to live forever, or to hold a dominant position for all eternity, nor even for a long period of time. They could die, they themselves could disappear from the face of the earth before reaching the full realisation of their civilisation.

SCIENCE

What is science? If you ask this question during the course of a more or less serious debate or conversation, you may feel that people are looking at you in a rather perplexed manner, as though to say: "What! You don't know!"

The dictionary will tell you: (science is) *a branch of knowledge requiring systematic study and method, especially one of those dealing with substances, animal and vegetal life, and natural laws.* Another definition: *Systematic and formulated knowledge in reference to nature, society, man and his thoughts, that is to everything which is the object of known facts which can be put to the test.*

In the encyclopedias we can find other definitions, deeper explanations of what certain philosophers consider science to be, the classification of the various sciences, the relation of science to mathematics, the distinction between natural sciences and those concerning man, and the relationship between science and technology. In this context I intend to consider the following concept: *science is a product of man*, it is created by men at a certain moment during the course of their evolution and maturity. Above all it is the creation of man who is advancing and acquiring more and more knowledge of the world and nature around him, it is a sign of progress. It is something which man himself has created. It is also a cultural message, an inheritance left to the world by a generation, a civilization, an inheritance which can be passed on to other developing civilizations. A developing society can absorb elements from a contemporary society which finds itself in a more advanced stage of maturity or from other past civilizations, and can then continue its advance, contributing, in its turn, to further progress and bringing additional values to those already existent. Science is culture. We can consider the expression *undergoing a phase of development* as positive in the context of a civilization, a particularly widespread social group, which is growing and maturing.

Other man made creations are art and poetry in general, civil institutions and all those material things which we commonly know to have been made by men, both by our contemporaries and by men in past epochs.

Science is, perhaps, the clearest indicator of man's progress, together with technology. A value added to the knowledge and the standard of living which had been reached up to its creation. Science as a creation of man is, at times, considered today as *absolute good* and has become the basis of an ideology. Science, it appears, has become a divinity. The human faculty which creates science, that is reason, rationality, is also wrongly exalted. The *Goddess Reason*, created by the followers of the Enlightenment at the time of the French Revolution was an idol created by the rationality of men, in which men were invited to believe, which men were invited to venerate. When discussing men, progress, science in general, I would suggest that the importance of man who creates and who uses science be underlined rather than that of the science he himself or other men have created or that of the particular moment in his historic evolution which enabled him to create science and technology. Without exalting man, without exalting man's creations, without considering man as God.

There is sometimes a tendency to consider science as something useful, something good, while poetry is not thought of in the same manner, especially in the circles of modern scientists who rate themselves superior to other men in the same cultural environments, superior above all literary time-wasters, but also superior to those politicians who understand nothing about science and those who do not put enough money into scientific institutions. The natural sciences, above all physics, are considered superior to the human sciences, superior to the arts. Who are the poets who read and write poetry in their cultural circles if not time-wasters? Who are the artists who paint such strange pictures, incomprehensible, real and proper caprices – compared to scientists who keep their feet firmly on the ground and who are expression of the power, of the efficiency and of the best realizations of man?

We must be careful. I would invite people to look at man in all his total aspects, through the eyes of a humanist, both man as an individual and also organized societies which evolve in time and then die and disappear. The humanist with his feet on the ground is a rational man, he himself is, too, a man of science. Amongst other things I would also invite all people, including those who are more specifically interested in science, to question themselves as to how and why man is here on this Earth. I myself feel the influence of the whole philosophy of history of the Western World, in particular that of G. B. Vico (1668-1744), a philosophy which anticipates and sums up all the German and European philosophy in the following two centuries.

One of his *"degnità"* says:

"Men first of all feel without knowing, then they feel with a perturbed and emotional soul, in the end they reflect with a pure mind."

This *"degnità"* summarises the behaviour of men in the various stages of their evolution within the civilization they belong to. First of all there is a phase where sentiments dominate, often irrational, with the creation of myths, of religions and of poetry – and later a more mature and more rational stage with the creation of philosophy and science. Consider the cultural environment of the Italian society in the period which follows the year 1000 up to and including the Renaissance, and some of its more outstanding personages:

Francis of Assisi (1182-1226): poet, founder of the Italian language and religious reformer who marked a decisive change of attitude as regards the religious living of his time.

Dante (1265-1321): summa poet and founder of the Italian language.

Petrarch (1304-1374): poet and founder of the Italian language, but a little more rational than Dante and St Francis; representative of a crisis in his time, he is still irrational but he is moving towards a more rational position, that of the Renaissance.

Leonardo da Vinci (1452-1519): artist but rational at the same time, affirmed proudly that everything he learned was fruit of his direct experience together with reasoning (we cannot say the same for Dante and St Francis).

Galileo (1564-1642): summa scientist, all reason, founder of an Italian language which is not poetic but prose, it is rational. Prose comes after poetry.

Shakespeare (1564-1616): summa English poet, creator of the English language. Shakespeare was born in the same year as Galileo, but it must be borne in mind that the two men lived in different cultural environments, in two societies which were at that time different: the full maturity of the Italian Renaissance, and late Renaissance for Galileo, and the first phase of the English Renaissance, with a delay of two or three centuries after the Italian Renaissance for Shakespeare, an epoch which corresponds to Dante's epoch in Italy. First of all Shakespeare and the Protestant Reform with the phenomenon of Puritanism, -- and then Newton followed by the Enlightenment and the Industrial Revolution in England.

In the cultural world of Greece, first we have the myths and the poetry of Homer with passionate irrational emotions such as the ire of Achilles. And also the religiosity of Achilles. In a later time we have the philosophy of Socrates and Plato, and the mathematics of the Greek mathematicians.

In India, first we have the poetry and the religiosity of the Vedas, then in a later phase, more mature and more rational, we have the philosophy of Buddha and Mahavira, and the creation of Indian mathematics, almost coinciding and in parallel with Greek philosophy and mathematics.

Science is a thing created by men, just like all the other things created by men: material things and less material things like poetry and civil institutions. Also: poetry and science are more interconnected than one may think: there would be no creation of science if in the very same human ambient there had not been creation of poetry in a previous epoch. Science is not created in the desert, but in one human context in evolution.

If there is a transcendent God, creator and Lord above everything, this is impossible to establish with our rationality, with our science. If we have precise data, if we have revealed data, then using our reason we can discuss these facts rationally. If man's behaviour is influenced by his belonging to a certain religious confession, to a certain ideology, then we can discuss this fact rationally. But if there is a God creator of all things, if He exists – this our reason alone cannot establish.

In this context I intend to consider the following concept: *science is a product of man*, it is created by men at a certain moment during the course of their evolution and maturity. Above all it is the creation of man who is advancing and acquiring more and more knowledge of the world and nature around him, it is a sign of progress. It is something which man himself has created. It is also a cultural message, an inheritance left to the world by a generation, a civilization, an inheritance which can be passed on to other developing civilizations.

Other man made creations are art and poetry in general, civil institutions and all those material things which we commonly know to have been made by men, both by our contemporaries and by men in past epochs. Science is, perhaps, the clearest indicator of man's progress, together with technology. A value added to the knowledge and the standard of living which had been reached up to its creation. Science as a creation of man is, at times, considered today as absolute good and has become the basis of an ideology. Science, it appears, has become a divinity. The human faculty which creates science, that is reason, rationality, is also wrongly exalted. The *Goddess Reason*, created by the followers of the Enlightenment at the time of the French Revolution was an idol created by the rationality of men, in which men were invited to believe, which men were invited to venerate. When discussing men, progress, science in general, I would suggest that the importance of man who creates and who uses science be underlined rather than that of the science he himself or other men have created or that of the particular moment in his historic evolution which enabled him to create science and technology. Without exalting man, without exalting man's creations, without considering man as God.

THE UNITY OF ITALY PATRIOTISM THE NORTHERN LEAGUE IDEOLOGIES

All those who distinguished themselves in some sphere of human activities in Italy during the nineteenth century were somehow also driven by a subtle sense of patriotism: love of the fatherland, of being Italian, politically and culturally. Different from and opposite to other Europeans. Not only the great contributors: Victor Emmanuel II, Cavour, Mazzini, Garibaldi and his followers; but also the poets, the philosophers, the scientists, the Catholics, and those who accomplished something if only on a regional level. Italian unity was brought about by a minority, made up of the highest and most cultured classes, before natural evolution brought forward the whole population, as happened later on, in the twentieth century. A minority, a new social class that was born with this sentiment, this ideal, and which had a decisive influence on the whole population in the next century.

This sentiment of love for the fatherland, a patriotism that would later become an exaggerated nationalism, is a nineteenth century phenomenon. After the experience of Napoleon, a center of interest was formed, a focus on which were concentrated all the best energies of a population, like an ideology or a civil religion that was both a spontaneous creation of men at a given moment of their evolution, and an ideal proposed by politicians around which all converged. Much like other nineteenth century ideologies. Italians want unity, they want to feel that they are a nationality like other European populations: *"Perché non siam popolo – perché siam divisi"* ... declares Mameli's anthem. This sentiment is a characteristic of Romanticism, even if a feeling of belonging – to a family, to a group – is natural to man and can be seen throughout history, though it wasn't as prominent in past centuries. In Italy, there are some distinguished precedents in the figures of Machiavelli and Petrarca, but little more. This patriotic sentiment later evolves into an exasperated nationalism for all the populations of Europe, and will lead to two world wars. *Nous les français"*, recite proudly the French. *"Deutschland Uber Alles"* is the German national anthem. Italy, too, wants to conquer and create an empire, like the other

European nations. When Italy believes itself strong, it attacks neighboring countries: Albania, Greece, Yugoslavia, France. Before the First World War, schoolchildren learned love of country – which should be good, a positive fact, one which creates cohesion and union. But at the same time, young people were being taught to be aggressive, to throw themselves at the trenches and against the machine guns of the enemy at the Carso Italian front. And the other European peoples were acting the same: some wanted to rebel against the superiority of other nations, and others who simply wanted to impose their ways on others because they felt it true and right. In two world wars.

This sense of patriotism and national unity emerged during the early period of Romanticism, with a new social class that was developing, made up of men who were distinguishing themselves in their areas. It strengthened in time, and gradually was felt throughout the nation – thanks to full scholarization, and to broader participation in public life, and reached its maximum expression during Fascism. The language had to be Italian, culture had to be classical and Italian, the Italian spirit had to be affirmed in every way. The culture of other European and extra-European countries was of little interest, not to mention the total lack of interest in local culture and dialects.

With the end of the Second World War, with defeat and suffering, the strongest feelings of nationalism begin to fade. People begin to speak of Europe more than nation: the European Common Market, United Europe. Exchange students begin to travel from one country to another, through Europe and the world.

At this time there are three exceptional men, all three practicing Catholics, less influenced by the ideologies of the century: Alcide De Gasperi, Robert Schuman, and Konrad Adenauer. At the same time in Italy we have the cultural phenomenon of Neorealism, with particular attention to the language and culture of the regions, and an Italian language strongly affected by local speech, no longer the exalted language of D'Annunzio.

The Italian regions are created, some with special statutes. Towards the end of the war, mention had been made of a free, independent Sicily. The ideologies which impose themselves on the political scene, Communism and Socialism, are the opposite of Fascism, they're of a more international character, less patriotic, despite later propaganda. Italian communists would like a large part of the northeast to go to Yugoslavia, a Socialist country, as the episode at Porzùs shows.

At the end of the twentieth century, when ideologies that had characterized the two previous centuries, as well as the sense of patriotism and national unity, had considerably weakened, new political parties with a regional character come to life – like the Northern League. Interest now lies in the life of the region, or a slightly larger geographical area, which does not coincide with the whole Italian territory with its capital in Rome (described as *Roma ladrona* – thieving Rome). Even the flag is derided. This new interest has an economic character. Many of the critics of the limited ideals of the Northern League act not only influenced by the magnanimous ideals of the past two centuries, but for simple economic motives. Or for political reasons; the noble sentiment of patriotism is used for electoral propaganda, to contrast those parties which seem to want to divide Italy.

The City States and Maritime Republics that brought Italy to the Renaissance are part of a splendid cultural and human history. Splendid also in an economic aspect-But it is a history of particularism, of small city states, and then regions, different from what was being formed throughout Europe with the creation of national states, which were destined to grow and influence politically smaller states. Even today we note the presence of strong nations, which dominate politically, economically and culturally. And we note the presence of smaller states. Some of these distinguish themselves for their economic efficiency- for example, Singapore – while others languish, and some split politically: in Africa, Asia, Europe. Europe itself, which had preeminence up to a few decades ago, in contrast to the great powers appears to be a geographical area made up of small unimportant states with no political voice. Which is better? Which is worse? To probe the subject more deeply and be able to comment, we must take up the discourse from a different point of view, and then ask ourselves some questions on why we live, act and suffer on this earth.

Today, Italian unity and patriotism are still values, even if we place them on a level quite different from that of two or three generations ago. And certainly an ideal remains, though that ideal is no longer absolute. For the generations before ours, one believed, obeyed and fought for the ideal. And was exploited. It was like a civil religion, another ideology – forced or proposed – but slightly more noble than the other materialistic ideologies of the nineteenth and twentieth centuries. All within the rather complicated context which is the story of humankind. Like life of man on this planet.

These brief thoughts can be of interest along the lines of G. B. Vico, as I attempt to analyze the concept by which *Man creates religion*, and therefore also ideologies and emotional and sentimental positions like love of the fatherland.

Some men distinguish themselves at the beginning of an historical phase and form a social class in a position of power. The great ideas, the great sentiments tend to evolve naturally and absorb the other late-coming social classes; they also tend to fossilize into civil institutions. With a radical evolution of society. Love of the fatherland, a spontaneous expression of man, an as an ideal proposed by leaders, can be more noble than many others, but it remains a creation of man; it is not absolute.

The 150th anniversary of Italian Unity was celebrated in 2011, an event which had never before received such solemnity. Many other national events had been and were celebrated: 4 November, anniversary of victory over Austria-Hungary, 2 June, Republic Day, 24 May, Declaration of war on Austria-Hungary, 20 September, Porta Pia, then the march on Rome, the birth of Rome, but **not** the anniversary of Italian Unity.

Was there a particular reason for this lack? Did someone have a special interest? Political, or simply economical? The attached essay suggests the evolution of civil institutions, to an evolution of collective sentiments, of ideologies and ideals. The ideal of *Patria* is perhaps one of the noblest that man can express, but in itself it is not an absolute, and someone could exploit this ideal to other ends: to gain political power, or more simply out of economic interests - so that the larger state will keep on its feet and continue to pay out pensions and salaries to civil servants.

Members of the Northern League sarcastically affirm: let's keep united. So that someone will work, produce and honestly pay all their taxes. Others in Italy don't work, don't labor, don't produce, and don't pay their taxes. Yet they gain benefits from those who do work. Let's keep united. Let's keep together. Love of the fatherland, of Italian unity – that's an absolute good. And it cost so much blood.

Let us not forget that the unity of Italy was made by a minority, by individuals blessed with magnanimous ideals. But that unity came about through violence, with the wars of independence. Initial violence has always been a founding factor of civil institutions, of laws of the state; violence with a good purpose. Even the Italian Constitution was written after that kind of violence- the *Resistance* movement. If followers of the Northern League want civil institutions to evolve in a way that favors their ideals of stronger regional autonomy, or even of secession, the strategy they have adopted will take them nowhere. Broader autonomy, or secession, with democracy understood as is, either with polite manners, or with insult of the flag and a low level of political intelligence like that of the Northern League politicians will go nowhere.

And again: the ideals of those who desire secession appear to be weak, even if they may be honest. It's youth that supports ideals. There are no young people in Italy and Europe today. Those who brought about the unity of Italy two centuries ago were all young and endowed with magnanimous ideals. Today there are no young people. Our population has aged. The birthrate, high, or low as we find today, is one of the determining factors in the evolution of civilization. A decisive factor in human history.

In the 1920s and 1930s many Europeans were attracted by ideologies, typically by communism: a humanitarian ideal to save the suffering masses. According to them, capitalism could not have saved them, after the economic crises. The ideal of a fatherland remains very strong. If we observe how single European intellectuals, be they Italian or British, are attracted to the ideas coming out of Russia, we can see a subtle resemblance to the fact that other men, in the sixteenth century, were attracted by the new ideas emerging from the Germany of Martin Luther. Human salvation could be reached through new ideas, not from the old structures of the traditional

Catholic Church. Many men believed strongly in these new ideas, in this new religion, and they fought and died for this. Or to uphold the previous religion. And some men in power were able to find space to maneuver within this new situation, acquiring political advantages by exploiting the behavior of men who were involved in the conflict, following religious ideals, which quickly became political. In the end, the abler politicians managed to bring together the vital energy of their countries for the benefit of their countries against other countries: Henry VIII, Elizabeth I, and then Cromwell. Like the European political leaders of the twentieth century, they garnered energy in favor of their country, against other countries, and the political ideologies, the new religions, collapsed on their own.

1914 - 1918 FIRST WORLD WAR

To the director of a Catholic Newspaper: Reading the historical books of the Old Testament, we find a recurring refrain: The chosen, the Jews, abandon their God, forge and worship idols, like the Gentiles. The Lord punishes them with war, famine, deportation. After a period of expiation, the Jews return to their land. To our emancipated eyes of the 21st century, these naïve and primitive tales seem aimed at children, characterizing a humanity that has since evolved and made giant steps in the fields of philosophy and science.

But perhaps the facts are even more serious. Feuerbach says that humans create religion through fantasy, through their own imagination, as they aspire to higher things, and not viceversa, as described so simply in Genesis. Vico said the same things with more substantial argumentation a century earlier.

Let us examine the First World War. This year we commemorate the centennial of the beginning of the war, and next year the centennial of Italy's declaration of war on Austria. For many years the date of this declaration was celebrated nationally, and almost religiously, as the expression of a poetic, patriotic hymn. Like a patriotic Easter, or Pentecost. Today this seems like madness to us, a collective madness that involves not only Italy, but all of Europe. The war could have been avoided with the simple use of reason. Today we don't love our countries in such absolute terms. In fact, in Italy there are political parties that deride our national flag.

Humans create religions. Humans build idols with gold, marble, clay, and they believe in these – as the psalm says. In the 19th and 20th centuries they stopped creating these material idols – perhaps the last was the Goddess of Reason of Enlightenment and the French Revolution. But modern ideologies are the idols now created by mankind. They are ideas, representations of human aspirations. They are good Socialism on earth, Communism in economy and human equality. They are Liberalism and

Democracy-as-the-supreme-Good, to be exported to Asia and Africa. They are love for the environment and nature, more than a baby who has yet to be born.

Francis Fukuyama says that the message Karl Marx directed to the workers and the working classes exploited by capitalists was the wrong message, in the sense that it arrived first as a patriotic message, then in a nationalistic manner, giving rise to the First and then the Second World Wars.

Mankind has abandoned God and has turned to other idols – the Homeland as supreme good before any real political ideology. And God has brought punishment: with two world wars, with mortal hatred between France and Germany, with suffering. In a broader context which shows that evil exists in this world. And we aren't able to fully comprehend all this. We can only realize that God shows compassion for those who suffer, like Job, and yet stay faithful.

EVOLUTION OF THE MORAL
SENSE AND PROGRESS

Observing the hundreds and thousands of years of history and prehistory, we can note interesting patterns of situations, even if not exactly identical, that repeat themselves over time, and in different environments. As regards the progress of mankind, or the progress of certain civilizations, of certain social groups, we have already taken note of the relationship between birthrate, fertility and material progress. Scientific, technological, economic progress, leading to conquest and supremacy of the territory, both in the technical, engineering sense and the political domination of other populations. Parallel to this first recurring pattern is a second pattern, that of the evolution of the moral and religious sense.

For the moment we shall ignore religion, the creation of religions, and we shall examine the evolution of a moral sense, or people's behavior. A moral sense seen specifically as regards the sexual sphere and sexual morality, and in a broader sense of attachment to work, to a social group, to a fatherland, to an ideal that can be magnanimous.

Throughout long periods of history, the moral sense evolves both from a narrow to a more liberal perspective, as a liberal to a narrow perspective : with prohibitions of behavior and attitudes that we today would consider obscurantist and irrational. Irrational behavior is a characteristic of mankind, both in reactionary and limited customs as well as in excessively permissive behavior.

Fifty years ago there was no miniskirt. Today there is, with all that follows. Moral behavior in Western countries has evolved towards permissiveness. To us in these countries, behavior that was suggested fifty years ago is to be considered obscurantist and irrational. And yet, we in the West are less important politically and culturally on the world stage than we were two or three generations ago. In developing countries, especially Muslim nations, the veil and the burqa were less popular then than now. When the

Ayatollah Khomeini was living in exile in Paris in the 1970s, he despised the *Parisiennes*, in his opinion too free and immoral. When he returned to Iran and became head of state, he imposed Islamic law, and the burqa and veil for women. Muslim countries have gained importance, in contrast to what they were several generations ago. Arab Springs, irrational aggressiveness with suicide terrorists, the hatred and contempt of the West, the strong attachment to their culture in contrast with the decadent culture of western countries – all these are elements that suggest an evolution of their moral sense towards a more restrictive mode. If we see this as irrational, it does not matter. To them, our customs, our moral sense, are irrational.

All the cultures on earth seem to have enjoyed scientific, economic and technological progress in the seventy years after World War II. In proportion, developing countries with a high birthrate and a strengthening of moral sense, even if not always rational, have shown stronger progress. Those cultures with a decreasing birthrate and ever-growing permissiveness, have lost importance.

When attempting to understand situations and historical facts pertaining to mankind, we must always be prudent. These two patterns regarding evolution are not exact science. Other elements have to be taken into consideration: the formation and development of social classes within a culture, as well as contact with other cultures. This could make it difficult to understand a particular phenomenon within a society. A social class could itself behave like a culture within another, larger culture. And it could even take on a leading role, or an opposing one, with the greater culture of which it is a part.

In Europe, after the year 1000, there was an upswing of civilization, the first sign of which seems to be the natural increase of population. Accompanying the numerical growth was the phenomenon of the heresies, and other religious phenomena such as the Crusades. The heresies are in themselves a sign of reinforced religious and moral sense. It makes no difference if they manifested themselves irrationally, or even violently, or if they followed the orthodox canons of the Church of Rome. The Cathars were violent, as was their repression under Pope Innocent III. The Reconquest of Spain had was of violent character. Saint Francis of Assisi, a giant for Vico, was certainly nonviolent. But he "perceived with an affected and perturbed spirit", and marks a whole era. He himself was an element of this development of modern western society, with its not very rational religious and moral sense. *En passant*, we note that, as the population grows and the moral and religious sense evolves, language and poetry develop, first in the south of France with the troubadours, then in Italy, with Saint Francis of Assisi. A real situation, this period of centuries after the year 1000, that can be seen in parallel with developing cultures in modern times.

The Protestant Reform of the sixteenth century represents a reinforcement of the moral and religious sense of developing cultures in northern Europe. In the "protest" against Rome, northern cultures strengthen their moral position against the corruption of Rome. It's not important if we note irrational behavior. It doesn't matter if several reigning monarchs take advantage of the situation for their own political gain. The same as in Asia today, and in developing countries. We can observe in passing that, together with the strengthening of the moral and religious sense with irrational manifestations, come poetry and national languages – important factors when studying history and the reality of mankind. In Switzerland, John Calvin exhibited an extremely high moral sense, but irrational, violent, fanatical and extremist to the eyes of the Roman church. In another historical situation that resembles that of the Reform and the heretical period after the year 1000, the Ayatollah Khomeini exhibits the same moral irrationality and aggressiveness. Strengthening of a moral and religious sense that are signs of progress of that particular culture, of that particular social group.

The American magazine *Scientific American*, in its September 2014 special Evolution Issue, The Human Saga, presents several detailed articles about the physical evolution of Humankind, with particular reference to the past fifty thousand years.

Scientific American
Special Evolution Issue Sept. 2014

I found your Special Evolution Issue, Scientific American, September 2014, extremely interesting.

May I express some interesting, and interested, considerations. I am not an archaeologist, nor a biologist. I am interested in human history from a comprehensive point of view, including the evolution of man and of civilizations, and especially in the relationship between **birth rate and progress.** This particular angle permits me to draw interesting parallels between your considerations in the evolution from seven million years ago, with the evolution of civilizations from the Sumerians up to the Greeks, to the contemporary world, with parallels with Indian and Chinese civilizations, and other minor civilizations. Also civilizations known only through archaeology. The historical parallels seem to be strikingly in accordance with your **Special Issue** considerations on pre-historic times. The ideas that I am herewith giving you in summary, are not completely mine. They were accepted tenets in history books during the years 1953-54 when as a boy I was studying Latin and Greek, history and philosophy of history. The Arab historian Ibn Khaldun (1332-1406), whom we can consider the Arabian Giovan Battista Vico (1668-1744), expressed similar ideas when commenting the history of the Arab and Berber tribes. If you think that these ideas cannot be accepted today in America, this may be due to modern day **ideology** which can be compared with bad **religion.**

Page 70. Article of John Hanks: *"Such rapid evolution has been possible for several reasons including the switch from hunting and gathering to agrarian-based societies, which permitted human populations to grow much larger than before. The more people reproduce within a population, the higher the chance of new advantageous mutations. Humans will undoubtedly continue to evolve in the future"....*

Page 72. *"dramatic changes in diet and a more than 1,000-fold increase in global population"....* Page 75. *"Even as medical technologies, sanitation and vaccines have greatly extended life spans, birth rates in many populations still vacillate."* ...*"Tracing the ancestry of human mutations gives us a tremendous power to observe evolution over hundreds of generations but can obscure the complex interactions of environment, survival and fertility that unfolded in the past"...* This may be the most important statement regarding the notion : **fertility = vital driving force in youth = progress.** It is not the high number of people per se, it is the vital driving force that is sign of high fertility and causes the population to grow.

Page 75. *"The power of random"*. Very interesting. Why not compare the notion of *"random"* in physically genetic changes, with the notion of *"Fortuna"* in the sense used by Machiavelli? The genius (Machiavelli means especially the genius in politics), is sometimes successful, sometimes he is not – perhaps a result of bad fortune, as happened in the case of Cesare Borgia, the son of Pope Alexander VI Borgia. The genius creates, the genius brings something new to humanity – if not physically as genetic changes: new things, new ideas, that is progress.

The article of Gary Stix reporting Michael Tomasello's pioneering studies, stresses the importance of **moral principles**, in the evolution, towards progress. Page 62: *"A collection of social norms required each individual to gain awareness of the values shared by the group – a 'group-mindedness' in which every member conformed to an expected role. Social norms produced a set of moral principles that eventually laid a foundation for an institutional framework – government, armies, legal and religious systems – to enforce the rules by which people live."*…

The article of Blake Edgar, page 48, stresses **monogamy**. Children are cared for by both parents, not only the mother. Cooperation, parental care, are one aspect of the evolution of the moral and religious sense. Evolution of the moral sense, together with birth rates, is a sign of progress.

The tenets regarding progress, which I borrow from history books and conventional wisdom seen in the fifties, are as follows – though not expressed in the very same way as I am doing here, when commenting new eras in history, and decadence in historical periods:

There are times in the evolution of civilizations when **the birth rate is high**, and there are other times when **the birth rate is low**. Progress, scientific, technological and economic, the subjection of the environment both with engineering works and as political conquest, political affirmation, always occur in relation to phases of high birth rates. Low birth rates are always the harbinger of decadence, of loss of political power, loss of scientific and technological knowledge, diminishing standard of economic life. High birth rates relate to the growth of the population, but the growth of the population is linked also to better agriculture, to better medicine. However, though important, these are induced phenomena, almost secondary ones (page 70-72). The main factor is the **vital driving force – élan vital,** that manifests itself in the youth of a civilization just as in the youth of an individual. In 18th century Britain, better medicine and agriculture permitted the growth of the population. Today, in western countries, excellent agriculture and medicine are not sufficient. **Life, the vital driving force** is the cause. Life of a single person and life of a larger community, of a civilization. Life begins, grows, evolves, creates things material and immaterial, and finishes. I know how it works, how it evolves. I do not know why. There is still something that I do not know in full. I keep to facts, to data. However, progress is not synonymous with happiness.

In civilizations there is **the evolution of the moral sense.** There is the creation of religions and ideals. There is the creation of poetry expressed with symbols. The moral sense evolves towards more restrictive positions, such as the phenomenon of **Puritanism,** with irrational manifestations. **Irrationality** is one aspect of human life. The moral sense evolves also from strict puritan positions towards more relaxed attitudes, like today in western civilization. In history, the reinforcement, the strengthening of the moral sense, linked to high birth rates, is a sign of progress, of advancement. The diminishing of moral standards is the harbinger of decadence, with loss of economy, of political power (page 62). Social behavior hypothesis, monogamy as a moral aspect, Tomasello's stress on moral principles – seem to be in perfect accordance with these considerations.

Social classes form, develop and decay inside the course of one civilization. The evolution of social classes, with eventual class struggle, shows a pattern of evolution similar to that of the entire civilization.

Complications**, interference** with other civilizations, simple commercial or cultural contacts, exchange of information may occur. Even from past civilizations to the present, as may be the case of Humanism in Renaissance Europe.

A genius who creates something new in the world, not only in science and technology, can be compared to a single random mutation in the evolution of the body. The concept of **Random** in evolution can be compared to the concept of **Fortune** in the sense Machiavelli attributed to historical happenings, and to the Prince's fortune.

The names to mention as the basis of this science of man are as follows: Ibn Khaldun (1332-1406), Giovan Battista Vico (1668-1744), Thomas Malthus, Charles Darwin, the philosophy of history in France and Germany in the 19th and 20th centuries, today's researchers and archaeologies such as those of September 2014 special issue of <u>Scientific American.</u>

I hope ideology, the media in America and elsewhere, will not prevent <u>Scientific American</u> from paying attention to this kind of information that is **human science.**

LAWS OF HUMAN SCIENCE

The September 2014 issue of <u>Scientific American</u>, about the physical evolution of humans and their technological and scientific progress in the past fifty thousand years, presents some important analogies and similarities with the progress of human beings in the historical era.

In my book (Angelo Bertolo <u>The Imminent Collapse of America and of the Whole Western Civilization</u>.... iUniverse Editor, Bloomington IN 2012), the following historical data can be ascertained, and the initial stances summarized.

Progress: scientific, technological, economic, environmental dominance, political. Creation of things, material and immaterial such as the arts and the sciences.

1   **High fertility.** High birth rate = **Progress.**

    Low fertility. Low birth rate = **Decline.** Loss of scientific and technological knowledge, lower standard of living, abandon of the natural world, loss of political independence when compared with younger and more vigorous groups. If the civilization hasn't disappeared altogether.

2   **Development of a more tolerant moral and religious sense = Decline.** Once there was no miniskirt, today, yes there is, with whatever follows (with displays of irrationality). **Development of a more restrictive moral and religious sense = Progress.** The Islamic hijab and burqa are more common today than in the past, in countries that have more political importance, and advance more than western countries. Reinforcement of a moral and religious sense as heresies and reaction to heresies, with political implications. (Catharism, the Protestant Reform, Puritanism, etc.). Momentous religious reforms. (With displays of irrationality).

3   **Men create religions** and ideologies, poetry and arts, philosophy and mathematics, science and technology, civil institutions, and all material things – at different times of human evolution. Then institutions tend to fossilize.

4   **Formation and evolution of social classes.** With possible class struggles. Some individuals, some families, emerge. They impose themselves on others. A social class evolves within a civilization, of a population which grows, and models itself on the civilization as a whole. Reciprocal influences with other social classes. One emerging social class struggles and imposes itself on the previous dominant social class – such as the bourgeoisie on feudalism, and lower proletarian classes on the bourgeoisie.

5   The evolution of one whole civilization can be compared to the evolution of one single person. One person is born, grows up, matures, dies. The sentimental intuitive time of a human being always precedes the rational time. Then the single human life comes to an end, at the old age of 80 or 100, but can die any time before, for any natural cause, or for any violent cause. Like a civilization after a pestilence, or military annihilation.

6   **Contacts and reciprocal influences with other civilizations**, of the present and from the past. (Commerce with faraway civilizations, Renaissance Humanism influenced by ancient cultures, by classicism.)

7   **Duration of a civilization.** A civilization can last for less than three centuries to more than a thousand years. A civilization can be defined also as an internal phase within the same civilization. A parallel can be made with a single human life: formation and birth, growth and development to youth, maturity, old age and death. Duration is not unlimited. Progress is not unlimited. A civilization, like a single human life, can end abruptly for many reasons: war, illness, famine and pestilence, etc. A high or low fertility rate is not a constant, but varies by its own nature.

8   Finally, after examining these facts, these parallels, we must ask questions about our **existence in this world**. I do not want to go deeper into this question.

9   **Observation:** who are they who most favor programs of birth control and abortion? Not Christians, not Muslims, not Hindus, not those who believe in primitive forms of gods like spirits of the forest. It's the Atheists, those who don't believe in God, who are not interested in God. They may be considered, or call themselves Christians or Muslims before a political institution, but in reality they are thinking only about their own personal interests, or the immediate interests of the Nation. In America, in Europe and in the richest and supposedly more cultured countries. With a permissive morality, becoming more and more permissive. In which countries are family planning and abortion most common? China, with its self-declared atheist, anti-religion leadership. In the USSR, before 1989, the Muslim eastern Republics (Kazakhstan, Uzbekistan, etc.) were less atheist, and less communist in economy than the western Republics (Russia, Ukraine, etc.), and the birth rate was notably higher. There was more food for the individual in Kazakhstan than in Moscow. And then what happened? The Soviet Union collapsed. Now we are expecting the collapse of America and the West. Viet Nam expressed its highest vital driving force fighting and organizing under the bombs. With a formidable 3% increase of the population under those conditions. And they won. Now the atheist leadership imposes a family planning program. Also Afghanistan shows a similarly formidable increase of the population.

Today only Iran seems to encourage fertility rates: with the declared purpose of doubling the current population of 81 million, with military and imperialistic goals. But also with simple confidence in life on this earth, and with a religious dimension. Fascist Italy and Nazi Germany both favored population growth, with imperialistic goals. The highest ideal for Germans was their fatherland, their superior race. An ideology which is a true artificial religion, an idol not made by man with matter, but an idea created by man. It took **two wars and much suffering to show that it was not true. (See: Man creates religions).**

THE NEW SCIENTIST
RE: *Enigma Variations, Sept 7, 2002*

The Seven Pillars of Wisdom

Significant progress in fundamental physics generally involves nature's constants in one of the following steps: (May I add: also in the human world).

REVELATION: We discover a new fundamental constant.

High and low birth rates, high and low fertility in one civilisation in different times, higher in the first, lower in the last phase. Also there is creation of myths, of religions; there is religious reformation, there is creation of poetry, men are more irrational and sentimental in the first phase, they are more rational in the last phase with creation of science and technology, of philosophy (Vico). Progress and power of a group, of a civilization, is in close relation with high fertility. There is little or no progress but decadence and death of that social group when birth rates are low.

ELEVATION: We discover a known constant to be more significant than we thought.

Yes, in the first phase of high fertility there is a phase of progress, of political expansion, of affirmation of one civilisation's identity in front of other civilisations, of creativity of that civilisation, of genius. There is decadence and loss of vital driving force in the last phase with a lower fertility, up to the disappearance of that civilisation, of that social group.

REDUCTION: We discover that the value of one constant is determined by the values of others.

More irrational in the first phase and less creation of new science. There is more rational drive in the second phase just because it is less rational by nature. Less poetic and less religious, but also in the very end less vital driving force in political attitude.

ELUCIDATION: We discover that an observed phenomenon is governed by a combination of constants.

Yes, the moral and religious sense grows in the phase of high fertility, wanes out in the phase of low fertility. That particular group or civilisation strengthens and expands its political influence in the high fertility phase, and declines in the low fertility phase. Creates poetry in the first and philosophy and science in the second phase as a general characteristic, but both are phases of growth inside a civilisation; in any case rationality appears some time before the lower fertility phase, before the decadence. One on the growing phase picks up elements from other older civilizations, part of the legacy of other civilizations. Some men distinguish themselves at the beginning of one phase for their human value, for their physical force, for their ability in business, for the level of their ideals, etc. They form an emerging social class that will be dominant for a time. This new social class will wane with the time, and will be supplanted by another social class.

VARIATION: We discover that a quality believed to be a constant is not truly a constant

There are variations in the long parabola of the evolution of a civilisation, with mixing phenomena, with internal complications. One person, one scholar, must have all the phenomenon in his mind and must use not only pure rationality, pure statistical data, to understand it, to grasp it. He must be endowed with some creative imagination, some intuition that goes beyond the stated rules, beyond the common thought of peers in academy, with some honest imagination, (not pure fantasy as with science fiction) even with the danger of being imprecise and not understood by peers. The constant of higher and lower birth rates in a civilisation is not always a real constant. Please note the heretical deductions of Copernicus that the universe does not revolve around us: he was condemned by the ideology of his times, like Galileo, by the scientific community – in addition and more than by religion per se. Today the scientific community in America and the media of Ted Turner unwisely condemn fertility even in America, against the general political historical economical interests of America. The people of these political and scientific communities are not endowed with higher human understanding: they believe in their pure reason only, they may be superb and feel superior. If there is an issue in America on fertility today, this is an issue that very much matches the issue about slavery in the 19th century: with sociological implications, with political and moral implications, and also with scientific implications.

ENUMERATION: We calculate the value of a constant from first principles, showing that its value is fully understood

Yes. In dozens of historical contexts I found these constants, although with complications, with the very same human characteristics. I think I understand them in a way most scholars do not dare to, because they are trapped in an ideology. This particular pattern repeats itself from the beginning to the end of a civilization, and inside the civilization at the beginning and at the end of the supremacy of the social classes that are arising and evolving. This pattern seems to be a very constant in different times, in different civilizations. If we assume this particular pattern and apply it to civilizations we do not know in full, as per archaeological excavations, we may consider it a known datum, an element that permits us to guess at and understand a little better that civilization. And the near future of civilizations that are present in the world today.

TRANSMOGRIFICATION: We discover that our supposed constants are a small part of a deeper, more universal structure

Yes, yes. We are talking about human beings, humans organised in living and evolving societies, with inter-related phenomena of a deeper nature. The first statistical phenomena I took into consideration was the pattern of Courses e Recourses of philosopher G. B. Vico (1668-1744), in the pattern of political situations to be compared in modern and ancient world according to Nicolò Machiavelli, but I discovered many other patterns on my own, or at least I strongly stressed other patterns that I found in the works of other people. Please note that Vico had less information at his disposal than, say, Hegel one century later, and that his are positive almost materialistic considerations. Still he is a believer, like the physicist today who studies the universe and the atom and still believes in God creator. Note also that unlike Hegel, Vico is more equilibrate and not a racist: his system does not at all consider the superiority of the Western Civilisation.

Please also note that in the very same wake of these seven pillars of Wisdom, with different kinds of statistical data in addition to the birth rates, considering patterns in the evolution of the (political and social) institutions, with two publications in 1984 and 1987 in Italian, I was able to almost exactly predict the fall (the evolution really) of the dictatorial regime in Russia and the advent of more democratic forms of government, and the loss of much of Russia's political and military prestige.

Fertility = power and progress
Genius and confidence in life -- human problems and paradoxes

Printed in the United States
By Bookmasters